WALKING WITH GOD

Book One: The Discipleship Journey Series

A WALK WITH GOD

Kevin Evans

Kevin Evans
Email: Kevin@cultivateleadership.org
Website: www.cultivateleadership.org

ISBN-13: 978-0-9830129-9-3
ISBN-10: 0983012997

Printed in the United States of America

Cover Designed by Li Yawen of SIG Design, Shanghai, China
Typesetter: Michelle Kenny, Fort Collins, CO

Dedicated to my wife, Lisa

ABOUT THE SERIES

The Discipleship Journey Series is primarily a resource to equip followers of Christ for spiritual leadership. Recognizing that effective leadership must emanate from the leader's personal life, much attention is given to becoming a person who wholeheartedly loves Christ. There are many people active in ministries who have learned biblical information, communication skills, leadership techniques, and organizational methods. However, the impact of their ministry is often lacking due to a deficiency of spiritual depth and maturity. What the world needs are spiritual leaders whose personal lives, character, and relationships have been deeply transformed by Jesus Christ. "Being" must come before "doing." Being a disciple of Jesus who continuously grows in His grace necessarily precedes doing the work of spiritual leadership. The person who increasingly responds to Christ in his or her personal life will inevitably influence others to do the same. This is the essence of spiritual leadership.

Ministry to others is the natural result of being a disciple of Jesus. My hope is that those who follow Christ as His disciples will intentionally serve as spiritual leaders, adjusting their priorities to His cause of global discipleship. My dream is to equip a generation of spiritual leaders who will help plant many new groups of disciples, especially in the major urban centers of Asia. In this way, we fill the earth with the fragrance of Christ. I have written the Discipleship Journey Series in hopes that it will be a useful tool toward accomplishing this vision.

Books One, Two, and Three are available in Mandarin (Chinese) and English.

Book One: *A Walk with God*

A Walk with God was written to help you discover the power of grace found in a relationship with Jesus Christ. Each one of the ten chapters takes you a step deeper into knowing Christ in a meaningful and life-changing way. Chapter titles with main Scriptures are as follows:

Grace	(Eph. 2:4–5)
Repentance	(1 John 1:9)
Worship	(Rom. 12:1)
Scripture	(2 Tim. 3:16–17)
Prayer	(Phil. 4:6–7)
Fasting	(Matt. 6:16–18)
Community	(John 13:34–35)
Meditation	(John 15:7)
Spirit	(John 14:17)
Power	(Acts 1:8)

Book Two: *A Change of Heart*

A Change of Heart is a ten-chapter book focused on how the gospel empowers you to overcome character weaknesses that often bring defeat. It provides practical hope for your transformation, which God intends to bring about by His Spirit and truth.

Book Three: *A Life with Purpose*

A Life with Purpose is intended to help you to confidently live out your faith and spread His grace in the key relationships of life: marriage, family, church, marketplace, community, and world.

TABLE OF CONTENTS

About the Series vii

Acknowledgments xiii

Introduction xvii

Chapter One 21
GRACE

Chapter Two 45
REPENTANCE

Chapter Three 75
WORSHIP

Chapter Four 97
SCRIPTURE

Chapter Five 125
PRAYER

Chapter Six 153
FASTING

Chapter Seven 173
COMMUNITY

Chapter Eight 199
MEDITATION

Chapter Nine 219
SPIRIT

Chapter Ten 239
POWER

Appendix A 261

Notes 265

About the Author 271

ACKNOWLEDGMENTS

I want to thank my Lord, Jesus Christ. He chose me and called me to come and follow Him as His disciple when I was utterly hopeless and useless. Now, many decades later, I remain utterly hopeless and useless apart from simply sitting at His feet, learning to live by grace. Jesus, thank you for the astonishing love, acceptance, and forgiveness you have given me in the gospel. I am overcome by the countless times You have comforted and encouraged me in those quiet moments spent with You. You continue to teach and remind me of the power of preaching the gospel to myself every day. You are my Joy.

I want to thank my most amazing wife, Lisa, and our remarkable children: Reagan and Amy, Rachael, Rebecca, and Rylie. The Lord was especially kind to me by including me in such a terrific clan. Their years of patience with my many flaws, forgiveness for my sins, and encouragement when I was low have kept me on the path of following Jesus. The love we share for one another is truly the greatest gift God has ever given me.

I want to thank my parents, Billy Joe and Noma Lee Evans, who have loved me and encouraged me to follow Christ in His ministry. My mother's daily, faithful time alone with God in Scripture and prayer has made an indelible impression on my heart. Her prayers for me have undoubtedly brought God's rescue and blessing to my life in unimaginable ways.

I want to thank the many people who have counseled, taught, and guided me to follow Christ. Even before I trusted in Christ in 1979, and every day since, the Lord has graciously intersected my life with all types of people who have contributed to my faith. May the Lord remember you and bless your acts of kindness for my benefit.

I want to thank Valley Creek Church, the fellowship God led me to plant and nurture for many years prior to our relocation to China. Their patient endurance and gracious support of me as a flawed leader allowed the Lord to make progress in the significant task of refining me to be useful to Him.

I want to thank the eighteen men who spent many months meeting with me in Shanghai early on Monday mornings to learn more of what it means to be Christ's disciples. The community we formed became the first to experience this material. Their devotion to the weekly gatherings, their commitment to learning from Jesus, and their courageous faith to make significant adjustments in their lives inspired me to no end. Their feedback greatly helped shape this teaching resource into a more usable tool for others.

I want to thank Zhou Jie, who gladly and diligently translated this book into Chinese. Her passion for the gospel and for China continually inspires me.

I want to thank Andrea Taylor, Ph.D., whose lifelong love and prayers for China made her and the team at *Third Chapter Press* the obvious choice as publisher.

I want to thank our *Cultivate Leadership* ministry partners who have faithfully prayed for and financially supported us since we began the mission. You have believed in the vision God has for us to equip the next generation of spiritual leaders for urban church planting. Your support makes this resource possible, and, in fact, this book is the fruit of your partnership. Thank you for sharing in our joy, and know that we love you beyond words.

INTRODUCTION – BOOK ONE

God wants a living, vibrant, love-filled relationship with you. He wants the two of you to share all of life together, and for you to know Him as your most trusted Friend, wisest Counselor, compassionate Master, and loving Father. He desires to be the passion of your affection, the fixation of your thoughts, and the longing of your soul. He created you to experience His all-satisfying presence as a daily reality. Can you imagine yourself enjoying this kind of relationship with God?

Many people want to know God but struggle to develop a genuine relationship with Him. The good news is that through Jesus Christ, God has made it possible for you to intimately know and enjoy Him. Following Christ is a journey, not a destination. Discipleship is not simply a Bible study course or a class you attend, where you eventually complete the assignments and graduate. Discipleship is a lifelong relationship with Jesus Christ in which you daily respond to His grace and truth. *A Walk with God* was written to help you experience a truly enjoyable friendship with Him as His disciple.

This book is like a map that guides you on your journey toward a meaningful relationship with God. In the first three chapters, you will learn to see God's astonishing love for you, to recognize your immense need for Him, and to understand how to respond to all He has done for you. In chapters four through eight, you will discover practical tools God has provided for you to strengthen your relationship with Him. In the final two chapters, you will learn how God intends to actually live within you by His Spirit. Each chapter ends with practical applications as well as group discussion questions to help you develop a close and loving friendship with God. If possible, gather a few friends and make this book the resource for a group study experience. Additionally, each chapter begins with a highlighted Scripture verse, which is representative of the topic. Memorizing these Scriptures will greatly enhance your spiritual growth. A complete list of the Scripture memory verses is listed in Appendix A. The pace of one chapter per week, combined with personal study, Scripture memory, and group discussion will maximize your experience. My sincere hope is that you will grow to treasure Christ above all else and that your *walk with God* will be your greatest journey. Let's get started with the first step.

But because of his great love for us, God, who is rich in mercy, made us alive with Christ even when we were dead in transgressions—it is by grace you have been saved.

Ephesians 2:4–5

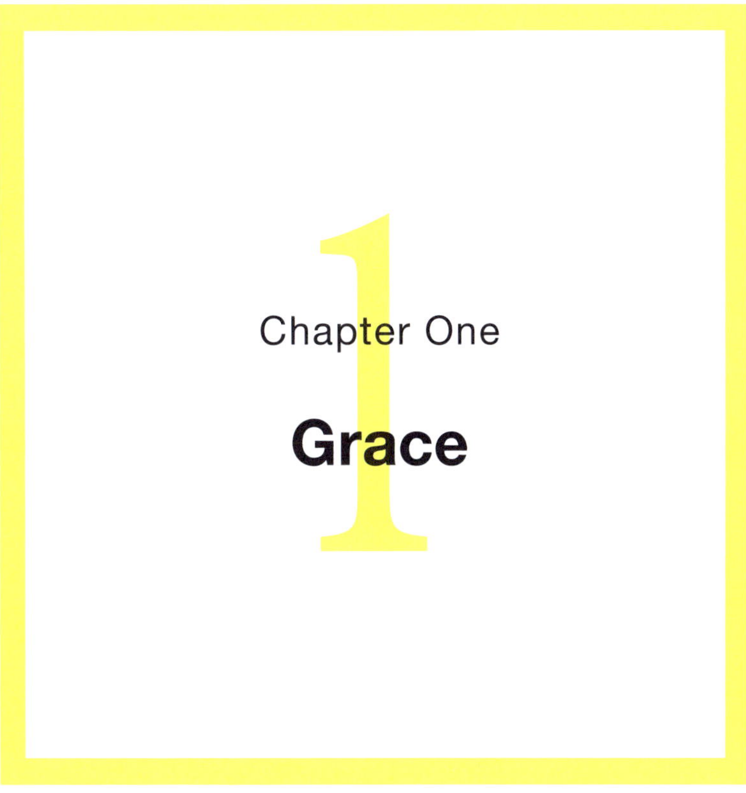

Chapter One

Grace

GRACE

I wanted to be the quarterback. I felt I deserved it. Although our rag-tag team of ten-year-olds was full of aspiring professional football athletes, I was confident that I was the best of them all. The problem was our coach—he did not see my talents and abilities the same way I did. He thought another boy would make a better quarterback, and he assigned me to block for him. Although insulted by the apparent demotion, I played the part and waited for another season to prove my high value. Unfortunately, not much changed the next year or the next. In middle school, I took up basketball, but with a similar result. I felt I deserved to be a starter, but the coach disagreed. During games, I spent most of the time on the bench, irritated that I was not getting the promotion I knew I deserved.

I was confident that I was the best of them all.

By the time I began my first career job, I had the same high regard for myself and was determined to prove my superior abilities to my company. Even though I lacked experience, I believed my credentials, education, skills, and winsome personality made up the difference. You can imagine how thrilled I was upon receiving an invitation to the annual awards dinner for upper-level management! The dinner was at an elegant hotel, and all were dressed in their finest outfits. Ten men, including me, were to be publicly honored and given a gift of appreciation. The particular gift that year was an expensive tie. As each man was called forward to be honored and receive his tie, my pride grew, anticipating the moment when my name would be called and I would receive my tie as well. However, something terrible happened. As the seventh, eighth, and then ninth man was called, I had this uneasy feeling that I would be overlooked. Sure enough, the ninth man was the last one called, and the event came to a conclusion. Not a single person present realized I had been overlooked—except me. Outwardly I smiled and greeted the others, congratulating them on their honor. But inwardly I was furious! I was angry with my boss, my colleagues, the company, even the hotel servers for this insult I had suffered. I simply knew I deserved better!

These silly examples from my life reveal my core problem: I think I deserve better than others, but the reality is, I do not. In fact, from God's perspective, I deserve nothing but death; the only reason I experience anything good in life is because of His grace.

Our True Condition

No spiritual life

Though all people are created in the image of God (Gen. 1:26), there is something intrinsically faulty in our souls. The Bible clarifies that the core problem for all humanity is rebellion against God, which results in spiritual death: "You were dead in transgressions and sins" (Eph. 2:1). God considers all people "spiritually dead." Though we exist physically, we have no capacity for spiritual life. Spiritual death means you are unable to respond to God or initiate your own recovery. You are completely incapable of responding to God's truth or God's love. In fact, you have lost your way and are alienated from the life of God.

Totally depraved

The source of our problem is sin. Sin is moral evil. It describes our rebellion against God and guilt from breaking His law. Though we occasionally do some good, and we are not necessarily as bad as we could be, we are nonetheless helpless to change our sinful hearts: "The heart is deceitful above all things, and desperately sick; who can understand it?" (Jer. 17:9 ESV). We are totally depraved, thoroughly perverse, and vile. It is as if we have a river of raw sewage spewing forth from our hearts. We are wicked in our core being; sin is in our spiritual DNA. We do not "become dead" because we sin. We are "born dead" in sin—born with a sinful nature (Rom. 5:12). Also, we verify our sinful nature by choosing to do wrong and by our inability to consistently do right.

Far from perfect

Some people may struggle to consider themselves as "sinners." For instance, I may compare myself to others and conclude I am not as good as some, but also not as bad; therefore, God must accept me. However, sin is not only doing "bad" things, like stealing, committing adultery, or murdering. Sin is also not doing the "good" things we should do: "Whoever knows the right thing to do and fails to do it, for him it is sin" (James 4:17 ESV). Sin is missing the mark of God's righteous perfection (Rom. 3:23). We are unable to meet God's standard of righteousness or do anything purely good: "All our righteous deeds are like a polluted garment" (Isa. 64:6 ESV). The Apostle Paul's letter to the church in Rome summarizes our true condition: "There is no one righteous, not even one; there is no one who understands, no one who seeks God. All have turned away, they have together become worthless; there is no one who does good, not even one" (Rom. 3:10–12).

"There is no one righteous, not even one . . . "

Rebels against God

Compounding our sin problem is that we follow "the ways of the world" (Eph. 2:2). Sinful humanity is bent toward selfish independence, which negatively reacts to God. The "ways of the world" refer to the godless systems of society that reject God's authority. It is an orderly rebellion against God in the systems of society: systems of relationships, economics, politics, education, religions, science, and entertainment—all of which are dead to God. These godless influences tempt us toward evil. Also, we are influenced by "the ruler of the kingdom of the air" (Eph. 2:2). The "ruler" referred to here is the Devil. He influences you to do evil in cooperation with your sinful nature.

Our sinful nature defaults to rebellion against God and our sinful actions verify we are dead, thus separating us from the life of God. Therefore, we cannot know, understand, or comprehend God. Because of our sin, we cannot have a relationship with Him. We cannot hear His voice, recognize His wisdom, or value His truth. Sadly, the world is a graveyard of the living dead. This sinful rebellion against God renders all people "deserving of wrath" (Eph. 2:3). God's integrity and justice demand He punish sin, and we certainly deserve His punishment. Even worse, we are incapable of ever attaining God's righteous standard and are destined for God's wrath. Our only hope is for God to bring us from death to life.

The Good News

God saves you

Fortunately, God has a plan to save and rescue guilty sinners. Though His justice demands payment for sin, His love absorbs the cost. God came to earth in the person of Jesus Christ to pay for our sin debt. Through Christ, we are brought from death to life: "But because of his great love for us, God, who is rich in mercy, made us alive with Christ even when we were dead in transgressions—it is by grace you have been saved" (Eph. 2:4–5).

God loves you

God's love for you is not based on your behavior, potential, performance, or worthiness. God's love is not dependent on the one being loved; His love is unconditional. His love motivated Him to die for those who ignored, rebelled, mocked, and hated Him. He is "rich in mercy" (Eph. 2:4). Mercy is not getting the punishment deserved. We deserve God's wrath, punishment, and condemnation for our sin. But God, fully aware of our evil hearts, withheld our punishment. He determined that He would not repay us for our sin. Instead, He absorbed the cost of our crimes. Rather than giving us what we deserve (wrath), He has mercy. God turned His wrath away from sinners and poured it out on Christ on the cross. Christ took God's wrath for us. This is the great miracle of the gospel.

"God . . . made us alive with Christ even when we were dead" (Eph. 2:4–5). As I lie spiritually dead in sin, completely incapable of responding to God or doing anything good, God comes to me and raises me to life! This is the gospel—God raising the spiritually dead to life. He took your sin-dead existence and made you alive in Christ.

Grace is undeserved

Remember, you did nothing to deserve God's mercy; it is entirely His initiative and His gift of love to you: "It is by grace you have been saved" (Eph. 2:5). Grace is giving what is not deserved. Despite our rebellious, disobedient, dead hearts, God gives us what we do not deserve but most desperately need: LIFE! Suddenly, you are awakened to God, and His truth makes sense to you. God's grace enables you to trust Christ, repent of your sin, and yield to Him! You begin to care about God and your relationship with Him.

Resting in what Jesus has accomplished

Not only does God bring the dead to life, He also adopts them into His family as His children (Eph. 1:5–6). He exalts sinners whom He has saved and cleansed to a place of royalty in Christ: "God raised us up with Christ and seated us with him in heavenly realms" (Eph. 2:6). God, in His grace, has raised you from spiritual death and seated you on

His eternal throne with honor in Christ Jesus. You begin your spiritual life with God by being "seated," which implies rest for work completed. Jesus Christ has completed the work for your salvation. You rest in what He has accomplished for you.

We display His grace

Why does God give so much good to people who deserve nothing but judgment? His purpose is that "in the coming ages he might show the incomparable riches of his grace" (Eph. 2:7). God displays the greatness of His grace to the universe by saving undeserving sinners like you and me. He raises you from death, adopts you as His child, and makes you His heir so that all will see His greatness. He alone deserves all the credit for saving us.

Believe and receive

Some might believe in Christ and experience His salvation by grace, but later think it was their effort that gained God's favor. Not so. We are "saved through faith—and this is not from yourselves, it is the gift of God" (Eph. 2:8). Even the ability to believe in Jesus is not due to our initiative, personal discovery, or innate spiritual interest. Faith is itself a gift from God that enables you to believe Him. God does all the work for your salvation. We simply believe and receive His gift. You are not saved by your self-effort, determination of will, or good works. Salvation is based completely on the finished work of Christ on the cross. There is nothing more God requires for His justice to be satisfied. He calls you to believe in Christ and receive His gift of salvation. As Jesus said, "This is the work of God, that you believe in Him whom he has sent" (John 6:29 ESV).

"... believe in Him whom he has sent."

An illustration adapted from John Piper[1] clarifies our true condition and Christ's saving work:

Scene One: You are suddenly in the middle of a lake, drowning. You cannot swim and are helplessly thrashing in the water. Then Jesus sees you struggling and throws you a life preserver. You splash your way over to it, take hold of it, and paddle to shore. You would be very thankful He threw you the life preserver. But you would also know that it was your splashing, grabbing, and kicking with that life preserver that saved you. You would be due partial credit.

Scene Two: Now suppose you have already drowned and are dead at the bottom of the lake. Also, what if you were the worst enemy of Jesus? Yet, Jesus dives into the lake, swims to the bottom, and finds you. He struggles to bring you up to the surface and onto shore. Then He works tirelessly to revive you so that when you finally cough your first breath of life again, He falls exhausted at your side and dies. As you come to understand what Jesus has done for you, you weep with gratitude, knowing it was completely

His effort and sacrifice that saved you. Then you hear a voice from heaven: "Jesus, my Son! You have given your life so others may live; now rise again to life!" Jesus rises and stands beside you. He takes your hand and pulls you up to your feet, saying, "Now that I have saved you and brought you to life, come and enjoy your new life in me."

The gospel is not God "helping" you, but God "saving" you!

If your view is Scene One, then you are assuming partial responsibility (and credit) for your salvation. You have not fully comprehended that you were spiritually dead and incapable of saving yourself. However, the gospel is not God "helping" you, but God "saving" you! Our true condition in sin (drowned at the bottom of the lake) makes the first described rescue impossible. We are so completely dead and lost, Christ must do all the work of saving us and bringing us to life: "Because of his great love for us, God, who is rich in mercy, made us alive with Christ even when we were dead in transgressions—it is by grace you have been saved" (Eph. 2:4–5).

Biblical Illustrations of Salvation

Adam came to life

Then "the Lord God formed the man from the dust of the ground and breathed into his nostrils the breath of life, and the man became a living being" (Gen. 2:7). Adam had no existence until God breathed into him the "breath of life." The Hebrew word for "breath" is the same for "Spirit" and "wind." When God breathed His Spirit into the man, he came to life. This is a picture of the gospel. Because of Christ's victory on the cross, the Holy Spirit comes into our lives and raises us from spiritual death into a new spiritual life.

Ezekiel and the valley of dry bones

The Spirit of God gave the prophet Ezekiel a vision and tour of a valley full of dead, decayed, human bones. Then the Spirit asks Ezekiel,

> "Son of man, can these bones live?" I said, "Sovereign Lord, you alone know." Then he said to me, "Prophesy to these bones and say to them, 'Dry bones, hear the word of the Lord! This is what the Sovereign Lord says to these bones: I will make breath enter you, and you will come to life . . . I will put breath in you, and you will come to life. Then you will know that I am the Lord.'" So I prophesied as I was commanded.
>
> And as I was prophesying, there was a noise, a rattling sound, and the bones came together, bone to bone. I looked, and tendons and flesh appeared on them and skin covered them, but there was no breath

> in them. Then he said to me, "Prophesy to the breath; prophesy, son of man, and say to it, 'This is what the Sovereign Lord says: Come, breath, from the four winds, and breathe into these slain, that they may live.'" So I prophesied as he commanded me, and breath entered them; they came to life and stood up on their feet—a vast army (Ezek. 37:3-10).

The life-giving, supernatural "breath" of God's Spirit brought a valley full of dead bones to life! This scene is a picture of the supernatural work of the Holy Spirit in the gospel—the dead come to life. God raises the spiritually dead to new life through Christ. He prophesies to us: "You, my people, will know that I am the Lord, when I open your graves and bring you up from them. I will put my Spirit in you and you will live . . ." (Ezek. 37:13–14).

Nicodemus must be born again

Jesus responded to the questions of Nicodemus by insisting that only through receiving new life will a person experience God's kingdom: "Unless one is born again he cannot see the kingdom of God . . . Truly, truly I say to you, unless one is born of water and the Spirit, he cannot enter the kingdom of God" (John 3:3, 5 ESV). Nicodemus was understandably confused, unsure of what Jesus meant by requiring a second birth. Jesus continued: "Do not marvel that

I said to you, 'You must be born again.' The wind blows where it wishes, and you hear its sound, but you do not know where it comes from or where it goes. So it is with everyone who is born of the Spirit" (John 3:7–8 ESV). Natural life, regardless of religious achievement, personal piety, or self-improvement, cannot experience God's kingdom. You must "start over" with a new life, only possible through the Holy Spirit (John 3:1–17). Jesus used an account from Israel's history to help Nicodemus comprehend the Source of the new birth: "As Moses lifted up the serpent in the wilderness, so must the Son of Man be lifted up, that whoever believes in him may have eternal life" (John 3:14–15 ESV). What is Jesus talking about? During Israel's wandering through the wilderness, the people rebelled against the Lord. The judgment for their sin involved poisonous snakes that brought death to many in the camp. Mercifully, God commanded Moses to craft a bronze snake, raise it on a pole, and then have all the people who were suffering judgment look up at God's provision. By looking at the snake raised up on a pole, they would be healed (Num. 21:4–9). Jesus considered this an illustration of the gospel: if we, dying under sin's consequences, will look to Christ and His payment for our sins on the cross, we will be healed and saved. We will be born again into eternal life (John 3:16).

Lazarus is called from the grave

Lazarus had been dead in the tomb for four days, and yet Christ called to him, "Lazarus, come forth" (John 11:39–44 KJV). The corpse "heard" the call of Jesus and was raised to life. In a similar way, we hear the call of salvation offered to us in the gospel. His "call" carries with it the power to believe and respond. And if we do, He gives His gift of life to us and we are raised from spiritual death. "I tell you the truth, a time is coming and has now come when the dead will hear the voice of the Son of God and those who hear will live" (John 5:25).

Ten Words Explaining "Grace"

In the next chapter, we will see how to begin responding to all that Christ has done for us. But first, take a closer look at God's grace. His grace is like a multi-faceted diamond; there is much to consider, and it takes time to appreciate its beauty. God's grace is an expression of His nature. As you reflect on each term that describes "grace," gaze into the beauty and love of Christ for you (Ps. 27:4). Recognize the amazing depth of God's grace expressed in the gospel:

Saved

"For it is by grace you have been *saved*, through faith—and this is not from yourselves, it is the gift of God" (Eph. 2:8).

Raised

"God *raised* us up with Christ and seated us with him in the heavenly realms in Christ Jesus" (Eph. 2:6).

Chosen

"For he *chose* us in him before the creation of the world to be holy and blameless in his sight" (Eph. 1:4). "You did not choose me, but I chose you . . ." (John 15:16).

Called

"God is faithful, by whom you were *called* into fellowship with his Son, Jesus Christ our Lord" (1 Cor. 1:9 ESV). "But you are a chosen race, a royal priesthood, a holy nation, a people for his own possession, that you may proclaim the excellence of him who *called* you out of darkness into his marvelous light" (1 Peter 2:9 ESV).

Redeemed

"For you know that it was not with perishable things such as silver or gold that you were *redeemed* from the empty way of life handed down to you . . . but with the precious blood of Christ, a lamb without blemish or defect" (1 Peter 1:18–19).

Forgiven

"In him we have redemption through his blood, the *forgiveness* of sins, in accordance with the riches of God's grace" (Eph. 1:7).

Justified

"But now the righteousness of God has been manifested apart from the law, although the Law and the Prophets bear witness to it—the righteousness of God through faith in Jesus Christ for all who believe. For there is no distinction: for all have sinned and fall short of the glory of God, and are *justified* by his grace as a gift, through the redemption that is in Christ Jesus" (Rom. 3:21–24 ESV).

Adopted

"In love he predestined us for *adoption* as sons through Jesus Christ, according to the purpose of his will, to the praise of his glorious grace, with which he has blessed us in the Beloved" (Eph. 1:4–6 ESV). "For you did not receive the spirit of slavery to fall back into fear, but you have received the Spirit of *adoption* as sons, by whom we cry, 'Abba! Father!' The Spirit himself bears witness with our spirit that we are children of God (Rom. 8:15–16 ESV).

Washed

"But when the kindness and love of God our Savior appeared, he saved us, not because of righteous things we had done, but because of his mercy. He saved us through the *washing* of rebirth and renewal by the Holy Spirit, whom he poured out on us generously through Jesus Christ our Savior" (Titus 3:4–6).

Sealed

"In him you also, when you heard the word of truth, the gospel of your salvation, and believed in him, were *sealed* with the promised Holy Spirit, who is the guarantee of our inheritance until we acquire possession of it, to the praise of his glory" (Eph. 1:13–14 ESV).

Projects and Practical Applications

Think through the following questions and write down brief answers to each one. Prepare to share your answers in your small group at your next session.

1. Describe your life before you trusted in Christ. (List a few one-word descriptions.)

2. What were three or four ways God "got your attention"? (Consider family background, circumstances, difficulties, relationships, and experiences.)

3. What are two or three Bible verses that have impressed you about God's plan to save you?

4. Since trusting in Christ, what changes has He brought about in your heart, your decisions, and your relationships?

- Change of heart (character):
- Changes in your decision-making:
- Changes in how you relate to others:

5. Why do you think it would be important to "preach the gospel to yourself" every day?

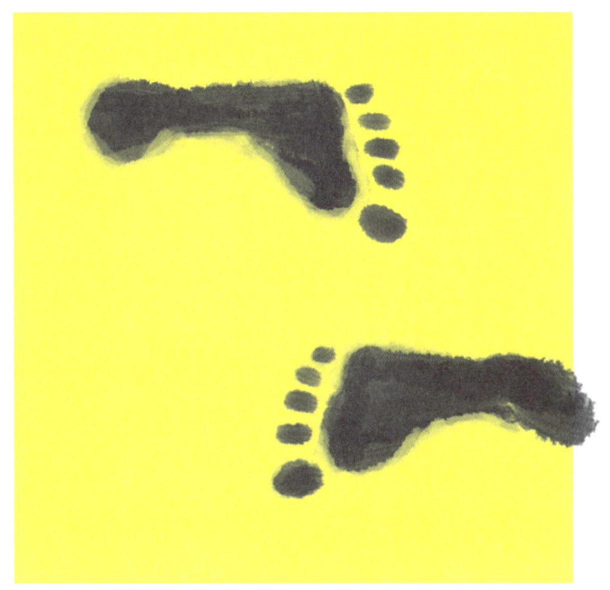

If we confess our sins, he is faithful and just

and will forgive us our sins and purify us

from all unrighteousness.

1 John 1:9

Chapter Two

Repentance

REPENTANCE

When I was fourteen years old, I was trying very hard to impress a particular girl in my school. We had begun a friendship, but I knew I was not special to her—she had not claimed me as her "boyfriend." One day I overheard my parents making plans to be out for an upcoming Friday evening. Their absence from home meant I would be there alone, with our family car parked in the garage. I got the brilliant idea to secretly drive my parents' car and arrange an official date with my soon-to-be girlfriend. I knew she would be impressed if I were to drive her in a car, on a legitimate date. One problem I had to overcome was to hide this event from my parents. The second problem was to avoid being seen by a police officer because I would be driving illegally as an underage driver. Fortunately, I was able to make my dream a reality: I picked up my new girlfriend, we drove to a restaurant for dinner without a problem, and then I dropped her back home and safely parked my parents' car in the garage. She was impressed, and I was proud of myself, having the thrill of getting away with something I knew was wrong. By the time my parents returned later, that same evening, I was home watching TV,

. . . getting away with something I knew was wrong.

acting as if I had been there all night. It seemed I had escaped any consequences of my actions and was a free man.

... the right to be the "boss" of my own life.

However, the next day I was surprised when my father came to me asking what I did the night before. I lied, saying I had been home watching TV. He then confronted me; he had checked the mileage on the car and knew I had taken it. My father was angry and disappointed with me, which caused me to feel ashamed. I quickly apologized and promised not to take the car ever again. But my father was visibly saddened that I had lied to him; he had lost trust in me. While he was obviously relieved to hear that I promised never to take the car again, he had to have been wondering if he could ever trust me again. I was punished and certainly regretted the consequences for my actions. Yet, as bad as my deception had been, there was a greater wrong that I was not admitting: I was unwilling to submit my life to my father's authority. Instead, I was reserving the right to be the "boss" of my own life.

God is Light

God sees your heart

We were created by God to enjoy an abundant life lived in harmony with Him. This joy God has for us is only possible when we respond to His grace and follow His lead. However, our hearts do not want to submit to God's leadership; we want to be the boss of our lives. Until we turn away from our rebellious attitude and yield to Him, we will have inner conflicts and forfeit His joy.

We cannot hide our rebellious attitude from God. His brilliance, purity, and holiness make all things visible so that nothing can be hidden from His sight: "This is the message we have heard from him and declare to you: God is light; in him there is no darkness at all" (1 John 1:5). Fellowship with God is only possible "in the light," which implies complete honesty and complete transparency: "If we claim to have fellowship with him yet walk in the darkness, we lie and do not live by the truth" (1 John 1:6). Everyone has sinned and missed the mark of God's righteous perfection (Rom. 3:23). Attempting to hide our sins from God by pretending we are innocent and going on with life as if nothing is wrong is both impossible and dishonest. "If we claim to be without sin, we deceive ourselves and the truth is not in us" (1 John 1:8). We end up deceiving ourselves and implying that God is lying about our true condition: "If we claim we have not sinned, we make him out to be a liar and his word has no place in our lives" (1 John 1:10).

Light exposes and reveals

When the Holy Spirit awakens you to your accountability before God, that is, coming into His

. . . you must choose to either "confess" or "hide."

light, you become aware of your sin. Immediately, you must choose to either "confess" or "hide." If you confess your sins, God is faithful to forgive you because of the finished work of Christ in payment for your sin: "If we confess our sins, he is faithful and just and will forgive us our sins and purify us from all unrighteousness" (1 John 1:9). Confessing your sin to God not only cleanses your conscience of guilt, it also improves your relationships with others: "But if we walk in the light, as he is in the light, we have fellowship with one another, and the blood of Jesus, his Son, purifies us from all sin" (1 John 1:7). Confession of sin releases you from guilt and empowers you to love God and others.

But if we choose to hide our sin—even though nothing is really hidden from God—we entangle ourselves further, and guilt results. We wrongly believe that we can get by with our sins, and not bring them out into the open for God to resolve. The Bible presents a number of examples of people who attempted to hide their sin from God, along with the tragic consequences that followed.

Adam and Eve

The serpent deceived Adam and Even into doubting God's trustworthiness and goodness. Their sin of rebellion against God broke their fellowship with

Him and destroyed their innocence. For the first time, they experienced guilt and shame. Adam and Eve attempted to hide from God and cover their nakedness by sewing fig leaves together (Gen. 3:7–9). Nevertheless, God came seeking them, to save them from eternal judgment.

Achan

Joshua led Israel to possess the Promised Land. Their first great victory was the dramatic wall collapse at Jericho. God clearly instructed Israel to take nothing from Jericho, but to destroy everything. But one man, Achan, secretly stole items God had forbidden. Achan buried the things in his tent and then pretended as if nothing was wrong. He wrongly believed he could keep his sin secret and that no one else would be affected. However, the next battle for Israel was disastrous because God had removed His protection. God revealed to Joshua who was to blame. Once confronted, Achan confessed his sin: "When I saw in the plunder, a beautiful robe . . . two hundred shekels of silver and a bar of gold . . . I coveted them and took them. They are hidden in the ground inside my tent" (Josh. 7:21). Achan's sin brought severe consequences not only on himself, but his family and his community.

Ananias and Sapphira

Ananias and Sapphira were a married couple and affluent property owners in the Jerusalem church.

They sold a piece of property to donate the proceeds to the church, hoping to gain the praise of their peers. They deceitfully presented the donation as if it was the full price, but kept back part of the money. Peter confronted Ananias: "'How is it that Satan has so filled your heart that you have lied to the Holy Spirit . . . ?' When Ananias heard this, he fell down and died" (Acts 5:3, 5). Soon, his wife suffered the same fate. Their attempt to cover their sin ended in a shameful death.

Inadequate Repentance

Feeling "sorry" about negative consequences

When experiencing painful consequences from sinful choices, a person is often motivated to change. However, the motivation may only last as long as the pain. Suppose a husband is unfaithful to his wife. His wife confronts him and then leaves him. The husband weeps over the loss of respect from his wife and his personal loneliness. He promises to be faithful and makes superficial changes. But as soon as the painful issues are resolved, he returns to bad form. Inadequate repentance only wants the pain to go away; the self-centeredness remains. There is no willingness to submit to God.

. . . no willingness to submit to God.

Jacob gained a larger share of the family's inheritance by manipulating his brother, Esau. Then Jacob lied to his father, Isaac, to secure a double blessing. Upon learning that his brother, Esau, was planning to murder him, Jacob fled from home. Twenty years later, Jacob hears the report that his brother, Esau, is approaching with four hundred men. Suddenly Jacob is filled with fear, and not surprisingly, has new motivation to repent. He sends gifts of livestock to Esau, hoping to diminish his brother's anger. He also begs God to spare him, spending a night wrestling with God, symbolic of his inner struggle to submit to God's authority (Gen. 32). True repentance must go beyond a desire to change the circumstances; it must lead to wholehearted submission to God.

Hating yourself

True repentance is not about hating yourself or trying to earn God's forgiveness by punishing yourself for wrongs you have done. Ongoing self-hatred is actually an expression of pride rather than repentance. It wrongly believes that "I should do better," rather than acknowledging my complete inability to do anything good (Jer. 17:9). This type of arrogance rejects the work of Christ as sufficient payment for one's sin. Self-absorbed guilt left unaddressed leads to anger and depression: "Worldly sorrow brings death" (2 Cor. 7:10). A proud, evil heart combined with unresolved guilt leads to depression and self-destruction: Judas "was seized with remorse . . . and went away and hanged himself" (Matt. 27:3, 5).

Refusing to remove sources of temptation

Sorrow over sin and a sincere desire to live righteously are important attitudes of genuine repentance. However, right attitudes must be expressed in right actions. If you truly want to avoid falling into sin, you must do what you can to purge your life of the sources of temptation. Nehemiah rallied the remnant to rebuild the walls of Jerusalem, and all the people then listened attentively to God's law. There was a wave of spiritual revival and repentance: "All the people had been weeping as they listened to the words of the Law" (Neh. 8:9). But unfortunately, the men of Israel continued to interact with pagan women and fell back into immorality and idolatry: They "have not kept themselves separate from the neighboring peoples with their detestable practices . . . they have taken some of their daughters as wives" (Ezra 9:1–2). Their tears of sorrow were not followed with avoidance of immoral situations and people. The Apostle Paul wrote, "Make no provision for the flesh, to gratify its desires" (Rom. 13:14 ESV). If your repentance is genuine, you will rid your life and environment of anything that leads you to sin.

Maintaining an independent spirit

. . . willing to obey God, but only on your own terms.

Inadequate repentance may bring regrets and remorse over sin, but not brokenness over pride. The focus remains only on the specific sins committed, such as anger, lust, or impatience. You feel sorry about what you did, and you earnestly want to do better in the future. However, the root cause of all sin, a rebellious heart that refuses to yield to God, is left intact. You are willing to obey God, but only on your own terms. You retain the right to be your own boss. You listen to God's input, but you reserve the right to make final decisions. You feel bad about your sins, but you intend to be god of your own life. This defines an "independent spirit." It is the same independent attitude Satan expressed that brought God's swift judgment: "I will make myself like the Most High" (Isa. 14:14). King Saul obeyed God's instructions for a battlefield victory. But Saul ignored God's prohibition and kept some of the best livestock. Saul justified his sin as a plan to bring an offering to God. But God did not want Saul's offerings; He wanted Saul's obedience: "To obey is better than sacrifice . . ." (1 Sam. 15:22). Saul's stubborn, proud heart cost him his role as king. Repentance must lead you to a full surrendering of your will to God. "God's kindness leads you toward repentance" (Rom. 2:4).

Genuine Repentance

Genuine repentance is inspired by God's love

Jesus told the story of a rebellious son who had squandered his family's wealth, ruined their reputation, and returned home pleading to be received as a slave. But the father not only forgave his rebellious son, he restored him with honor, wealth, and celebration. The father expressed his love for the son who returned home: "This son of mine was dead and is alive again; he was lost and is found" (Luke 15:24). This expresses the heart of God; He loves His children regardless of what they do wrong. Knowing that God loves you despite your sin is a powerful motivation to return to Him.

Repentance is recognizing that despite His great love for you, you chose to rebel against God. You consider that your sin has violated your relationship with Him, and you miss the closeness of fellowship with Him. You remember His great love for you and are drawn to return: "For if, when we were God's enemies, we were reconciled to him through the death of his Son, how much more, having been reconciled, shall we be saved through his life!" (Rom. 5:10). Apart from the unconditional love of God, true repentance is simply not possible.

Genuine repentance surrenders completely to God

Repentance is about changing direction, turning around, and adjusting your thinking. The basis of all sin is demanding to be in charge of your own life. Sin is rejecting God's authority and is rooted in pride and unbelief (Gen. 3:5). Every sin is ultimately an act of defiance against God and His authority in your life. Therefore, genuine repentance must address this deep issue of the rebellious heart.

"Have mercy on me, O God, according to your unfailing love; according to your great compassion blot out my transgressions. Wash away all my iniquity and cleanse me from my sin. For I know my transgressions, and my sin is always before me. Against you, you only, have I sinned and done what is evil in your sight" (Ps. 51:1–4).

Genuine repentance feels sorrow over grieving God

Repentance allows you to see your past from God's perspective and to recognize your selfishness, pride, and rebellion. You are able to reflect on how your sin has brought suffering to others, damaged your relationships, diminished your productivity, and stained the reputation of Christ. As you acknowledge the ugliness of your selfish motives and arrogant actions, you should be grieved over your sin. In addition to the hurt we bring ourselves and others when we sin, we also grieve the Holy Spirit (Eph. 4:30). Even though your relationship with God is forever secure because of the finished work of Christ, your fellowship with Him is damaged by sin. This recognition should bring sorrow to your heart: "See what this godly sorrow has produced in you: what earnestness, what eagerness to clear yourselves, what indignation, what alarm, what longing, what concern, what readiness to see justice done" (2 Cor. 7:11).

Genuine repentance confesses specific sins to God

If we are sincere in our desire to turn away from sin, we must acknowledge that we have actually committed the sin. We commit specific sins; therefore, we should confess them specifically to God. Generalized confessions, like "God, I'm sorry if I have done anything wrong," do not take responsibility for sin. Unless you recognize the specific sins you have committed, you will never repent or gain freedom from them.

King David lusted for Bathsheba and, tragically, committed adultery with her. After discovering she was pregnant, David arranged to have her husband, Uriah, killed in battle. However, David did not confess his sins to God, but continued life as normal for many months. God mercifully sent the prophet Nathan to expose David's adultery and murder. We read in

Psalm 51 how David finally took responsibility for his sins and confessed them to God:

> Have mercy on me, O God, according to your steadfast love; according to your abundant mercy blot out my transgressions. Wash me thoroughly from my iniquity, and cleanse me from my sin! For I know my transgressions, and my sin is ever before me. Against you, you only, have I sinned and done what is evil in your sight, so that you may be justified in your words and blameless in your judgment (Ps. 51:1–4 ESV).

Genuine repentance takes action

Repentance is a change of life. If there is no change of life, there was no true repentance. You cannot hide repentance; it will eventually be expressed in the way you think, speak, and act. Simply "going through the motions" of verbal confession without submitting your life to the Lordship of Christ is pointless. As Jesus said, "Why do you call me, 'Lord, Lord,' and do not do what I say?" (Luke 6:46). Zacchaeus, a corrupt tax collector, had always been the boss of his own life. But his encounter with Jesus led him to submit himself, and his idol of money, to Christ: "Look, Lord! Here and now I give half of my possessions to the poor, and if I have cheated anybody out of anything, I will pay back four times the amount" (Luke 19:8).

Why Repentance Matters

Repentance displays the grace of God

Every time someone repents, it reveals God's love. No one repents because of his or her own good intentions or initiative. Repentance is always a response to the goodness of God. Peter had spent his life as a fisherman, accumulating a large catch of sins. When Jesus revealed His divine power by giving Peter an overwhelming catch of fish, Peter broke down: "He fell at Jesus' knees and said, 'Go away from me, Lord; I am a sinful man!'" (Luke 5:8). The overwhelming catch of fish was a picture of God's abundant grace for Peter, and Peter's overwhelming repentance made God's grace visible to others. God's love motivates me to repent, choose His way, and redirect my life to follow Him.

Repentance restores your fellowship with God

When your fellowship with God has been broken because of sin, only repentance will fully restore you to Him in a close, meaningful way. It is intrinsic to the gospel for sinners to repent (Luke 24:47; Acts 2:38). Without repentance, a person may continue learning about God and doing religious activities but make no spiritual progress in faith or character. An unrepentant, self-righteous Christian is nauseating to Jesus (Rev. 3:16). Jesus told a story of two men who went to pray: one, a law-abiding Pharisee, and the other, a remorseful tax collector. The Pharisee used prayer to boast about his personal accomplishments, but the tax collector humbled himself. He "stood at a distance. He would not even look up to heaven, but beat his breast and said, 'God, have mercy on me, a sinner.' I tell you that this man, rather than the other, went home justified before God" (Luke 18:13–14).

Repentance clears your conscience

No one *earns* forgiveness from God by repenting or confessing sins. Only the blood of Jesus satisfies the justice of God. Christ has permanently covered your sins, and God views you as clean in His sight (1 Peter 1:19). Because of the finished work of Christ, your sins (past, present, and future) are already forgiven in God's sight: God is "not counting men's sins against them" (2 Cor. 5:19).

However, when you sin, you violate your conscience, which results in guilt. You know something is wrong in your fellowship with God, and you are eager to make it right: "Then I acknowledged my sin to you and did not cover up my iniquity. I said, 'I will confess my transgressions to the Lord'—and you forgave the guilt of my sin" (Ps. 32:5). Only by genuine repentance will your conscience be free, allowing you to feel God's love and acceptance. "Let us draw near to God with a sincere heart in full assurance of faith, having our hearts sprinkled to cleanse us from a guilty conscience . . ." (Heb. 10:22).

Repentance aligns you with the purposes of God

To confess is to agree with God about a matter. So confessing sin is saying the same thing about it as God says about it. We agree with our Father that our behavior and attitude are wrong; that we were selfish or lustful or unloving. Confession agrees with God that we have rebelled against His leadership in our lives. The process of our spiritual healing begins during this moment of agreement with God. Jesus made repentance the starting point for His rule in one's life: "Repent, for the kingdom of heaven is near" (Matt. 4:17). Martin Luther's famous posting of the ninety-five theses began with this first statement on his list: "The entire life of the believer should be one of repentance." The more closely we walk with Christ, the more aware we become when we have grieved Him. Knowing we have grieved our Lord should quickly lead us to repent and align our lives with Him.

To confess is to agree with God.

Repentance renews your fellowship with others

Sin not only hurts you, but it also damages every relationship in your life. Sometimes we are not even aware that our sinful attitudes and actions wound others. But repentance creates an urgency to make things right with those whom you have wronged by your sin. "But if we walk in the light, as he is in the light, we have fellowship with one another, and the blood of Jesus, his Son, purifies us from all sin" (1 John 1:7). Repentance sets you free from pretending to be righteous, or having to win every argument, or always defending yourself, or exposing the failures of others. Repentant people are joyful in their repentance; there is freedom to no longer carry the guilt, grudge, or anger: "I was wrong; I should never have done that, please forgive me. Let's make it right."

Repentance brings joy to the heart of God

Repentance is coming home to your heavenly Father who created you and loves you. He delights to receive His sons and daughters who return to Him. Every time you respond to God's grace by turning your life in His direction, it brings joy to His heart. There is an unseen heavenly audience watching, waiting, and celebrating your repentance: "There is rejoicing in the presence of the angels of God over one sinner who repents" (Luke 15:10).

Projects and Practical Applications

1. Take a personal inventory. One of the most revealing experiences you will have in your spiritual journey is to recognize the sins in your life. To take inventory is to honestly examine, with the guidance of the Holy Spirit, the sins that frequently defeat you. An extensive list of sins is provided here as a tool to help you assess your condition. This exercise will help you see, in specific terms, the violations of God's Ten Commandments (Ex. 20:1–17). In preparation for this self-appraisal, do the following:

2. Set aside time to work through the inventory and thoughtfully consider your life with the guidance of the Holy Spirit. Identify the areas of sin that have defeated you or are currently a problem and then anticipate the future victories you will experience in Christ.

3. Be completely honest with yourself and with God, because total honesty is the key to success. How free do you want to be? Avoid wasting your time with denial, pretense, or superficiality.

4. Talk it over with God. Come humbly before the Lord in prayer, confident that He is the One who started this good work in you, and He will complete it (Phil. 1:6). Ask the Lord to bring to memory the names of people, groups, institutions, and situations that have negatively affected your life. Let Him lead you to deeply repent of all things that hinder your relationship with Him.

5. When you have settled into a quiet place and have connected meaningfully with the Lord, you are then ready to begin your inventory. Prayerfully read through the list, searching your heart and listening for the promptings of the Spirit to repent. The process of identifying specific sins can be helpful because a hardened heart will sometimes feel no guilt even though sin is present. Obviously, this list refers to sins you have committed yourself, or against others—not sins committed against you (e.g., incest). You are not to blame and, therefore, do not need to repent for the sins that have been committed against you. However, be attentive to the issues from your past that may be buried and somewhat forgotten. Sin left unresolved does not go away and, in fact, will continue to defeat you. Repentance uproots these "weeds" from bringing further damage to your life.

6. Accept brokenness as God's way of working in your life. The inventory is similar to a farmer plowing hardened ground, preparing the soil to receive seeds and produce a greater harvest. Like a farmer plowing his fields for planting, you only need to go through this extensive exercise rarely. Take time to allow the plow of God's truth and Spirit to break up the hardened areas of your heart. Evaluate the areas where you have failed in your past, are regularly defeated now, or are struggling for victory. Circle all the ones that apply to you. Then spend time reflecting on how your sin has grieved the Holy Spirit, damaged your relationships, and wounded your own soul. Allow your heart to be broken by your rebellion against God. Repent by confessing each sin to God and by thanking Him for the sacrifice of Jesus, who paid for your forgiveness. Meditate on His amazing grace and unconditional love for you in Isaiah 53:4-6:

> Surely he took up our infirmities and carried
> our sorrows,
> yet we considered him stricken by God,
> smitten by him, and afflicted.
> But he was pierced for our transgressions,
> he was crushed for our iniquities;
> the punishment that brought us peace was on him,
> and by his wounds we are healed.
> We all, like sheep, have gone astray,
> each of us has turned to his own way;
> and the Lord has laid on him
> the iniquity of us all.

Inventory of personal sins

Pride:

- ❑ Arrogance; conceit
- ❑ Control or manipulation of others
- ❑ Defensiveness
- ❑ Dishonesty; lying
- ❑ Excessive criticism of others
- ❑ Gripes and complaints
- ❑ Laziness
- ❑ Profanity
- ❑ Rebellion toward authority
- ❑ Self-righteousness
- ❑ Selfish ambition
- ❑ Selfishness

Anger:

- ❑ Angry outbursts
- ❑ Bitterness, unforgiveness
- ❑ Emotional withdrawal from others
- ❑ Gossip or slander
- ❑ Grudges
- ❑ Hatred
- ❑ Hopelessness
- ❑ Jealousy
- ❑ Murder

- ❑ Self-hatred
- ❑ Self-pity
- ❑ Violence

Greed:

- ❑ Discontentment
- ❑ Envy
- ❑ Excessive shopping
- ❑ Gambling
- ❑ Hoarding
- ❑ Theft
- ❑ Drunkenness; excessive drinking
- ❑ Gluttony; overeating

Fears:

- ❑ Fear of trusting God
- ❑ Fear of abandonment
- ❑ Fear of aging
- ❑ Fear of conflict or confrontation
- ❑ Fear of change
- ❑ Fear of death
- ❑ Fear of financial need
- ❑ Fear of illness
- ❑ Fear of intimacy in relationships
- ❑ Fear of losing a loved one in death
- ❑ Fear of losing control

- ❑ Fear of pain
- ❑ Fear of people in authority
- ❑ Fear of personal weaknesses being exposed
- ❑ Fear of rejection
- ❑ Fear of success or failure
- ❑ Fear of the unknown or future

Immorality:

- ❑ Adultery
- ❑ Bestiality
- ❑ Homosexuality
- ❑ Immoral fantasizing
- ❑ Incest
- ❑ Lust
- ❑ Pornography
- ❑ Premarital sex
- ❑ Promiscuity
- ❑ Prostitution
- ❑ Self-sex, or masturbation

False Religions:

- ❑ Non-Christian, religious cults
- ❑ Binding covenants (fraternities, sororities, freemasonry)
- ❑ Binding ideologies (atheism, humanism, Marxism, Scientology)

- ❑ Non-Christian forms of worship (Baha'i, Buddhism, Hinduism, Islam, New Age)
- ❑ Idolatry (Buddhist idols, Catholic saints, Mariolatry, Hindu idols)
- ❑ Occult experiences (astrology, magic, clairvoyance, fetishism, fortune-telling, palm reading, psychic beliefs, psychic healing, Satanism, séance, hypnosis)
- ❑ Witchcraft

Small group discussion:

1. As a group, each one should commit to absolute confidentiality. Apart from this agreement, trust cannot develop within the group and sharing will remain superficial. Begin your group discussion by making this commitment to one another.

2. Share honestly and appropriately with your group some of your past areas of failure. Honest, humble confession is a powerful tool of accountability and freedom that leads to victory. Avoid excessive details, but do not let pride prevent you from humbly acknowledging the things you have done wrong. Confessing your sins to one another is a powerful act of humility that brings supernatural benefits (Prov. 28:13; Acts 19:18; James 5:16).

Therefore, I urge you, brothers and sisters, in view of God's mercy, to offer your bodies as a living sacrifice, holy and pleasing to God—this is your true and proper worship.

Romans 12:1

Chapter Three

Worship

WORSHIP

Over the course of your life, what have been the activities, possessions, and plans that have been most important to you? Also, who are the very special people you would say have been at the center of your life? When I entered high school, the most important thing in life to me was football. I was quite proud to be included on our school team and worked hard to excel among my teammates. Not surprisingly, I considered the football coach's opinion of me of ultimate importance. I thought about football, talked about football, and dreamed about football. I read sportswriters' reports on football teams and spent much time watching football games on TV. If someone were to watch my life for only a short time, they would easily conclude that football was the most important thing in my life. I believed football gave my life meaning and happiness.

> *. . . football was the most important thing in my life.*

Later, however, I had a new interest—I wanted a car. I was certain that owning a car would make me popular with my friends and give me the feeling of independence, freedom, and power. For many years, I had saved money for this purchase, and my father helped me find a suitable, used car to buy. I was exceedingly proud to have a car of my own and spent much time cleaning the car, repairing the car, driving the car, and talking to others about my car. The car was constantly on my mind.

Eventually, as a university student, my focus shifted to finding a girlfriend. I was convinced that having a special girlfriend would make me feel secure and happy. I met a wonderful young woman named Lisa, who later became my wife. While we were dating, I was consumed with Lisa and wanted to spend every available minute with her. Whether I was in class or studying or working, I was thinking about her. We did eventually get married and yet, my heart began seeking fulfillment with another new goal. I turned my focus to earning a graduate degree. I poured all my energies into my studies and believed the advanced degree would give my life significance. Once I graduated, I pursued a job, believing it would fulfill my longings for purpose and meaning. I worked diligently, striving to advance in my career. My career became the center of my life. Later, there were more things that captured my imagination and time, including buying a home, having children, and acquiring various possessions.

I was convinced that having a special girlfriend would make me feel secure and happy.

Why is it that we behave like this? We do this because we are created to focus on something or someone we believe will give our lives significance, security, and happiness. This consuming focus is not something we strive to do; it is simply our reality. The truth is that we attribute ultimate worth to whatever we believe will fill our emptiness of heart. This is worship, and you are a worshipper. We are always worshipping something or someone, seeking to fill our emptiness with various activities, possessions, and relationships. Yet even these good things cannot meet our deepest need. We were made for Someone greater; we were made for God. The French philosopher, Blaise Pascal, wrote, "There is a God-shaped vacuum in the heart of every man which cannot be filled by any created thing, but only by God, the Creator, made known through Jesus."

God's Word Speaks of Worship

Biblical descriptions of worship

The Bible has much to say about worship. Consider the reverence that influenced the psalmist who wrote: "Come, let us bow down in worship, let us kneel before the Lord our Maker" (Ps. 95:6). To worship is to acknowledge God's true worth and then respond appropriately with admiration, honor, and devotion: "Ascribe to the Lord the glory due his name; worship the Lord in the splendor of his holiness" (Ps. 29:2).

When we recognize His true beauty, we naturally want to praise Him: "Oh come, let us sing to the Lord; let us make a joyful noise to the rock of our salvation! Let us come into his presence with thanksgiving; let us make a joyful noise to him with songs of praise! For the Lord is a great God, and a great King above all gods . . . Oh come, let us worship and bow down; let us kneel before the Lord, our Maker!" (Ps. 95:1–3, 6–7 ESV). Louie Giglio[2] says: "Worship is our response, both personal and corporate, to God for who He is, and what He has done; expressed in and by the things we say and the way we live." God's joy flows from His infinite beauty and greatness. There is no one who surpasses Him in any truly admirable trait. He is absolutely enjoyable. "You will fill me with joy in your presence" (Ps. 16:11). And in the Old Testament, God prescribed the place and practice of worship. While on the wilderness journey, God directed Israel to worship at the tabernacle, which was the specially designed Tent of Meeting. Once settled in Jerusalem, the temple was constructed and became the central place of worship. The location, structure, elements, and sacrifices were all signs pointing to the ultimate reality that would be fulfilled in Jesus Christ. Jesus also taught on the value of worship. He stated that His Father seeks those who "will worship the Father in Spirit and truth" (John 4:23). The term "worship" in this context means, "to kiss toward." Worship is an expression of affection to God, in response to discovering His great value.

Jesus expressed His immeasurable value in this short story: "A merchant in search of fine pearls, who, on finding one pearl of great value, went and sold all that he had and bought it" (Matt. 13:45–46 ESV).

Worship in action

Worship is not simply believing in God. It is recognizing His true value and then gladly adjusting all of what you know of yourself to all you know of Him. Mary was one who grasped the infinite value of Christ: "Mary took about a pint of pure nard, an expensive perfume; she poured it on Jesus' feet and wiped his feet with her hair. And the house was filled with the fragrance of the perfume (John 12:3). Jesus said regarding Mary: "Wherever the gospel is preached throughout the world, what she has done will also be told, in memory of her'" (John 12:3; see also Mark 14:3–9). Mary's extravagant gift demonstrated how deeply she valued Jesus. This is what the gospel produces: people who gladly give all they have to Jesus because they recognize His true value. Jesus Christ did for us what we could not do for ourselves when He was crucified on the cross: "Christ died for sins once for all, the righteous for the unrighteous, to bring us to God" (1 Peter 3:18). This is why the gospel fuels our worship. Jesus absorbed God's wrath against our sin and opened the way for us to truly recognize His beauty and value. Because of this, we treasure Him. For you to have the ability to hear, to appreciate, and then to respond to God's call cost Him the life of His Son. Therefore, for God to call you to worship Him is the most loving thing He could do for you. When complete attention is focused on God (in the gospel), you experience your greatest joy. Theologian D. A. Carson[3] writes: "To worship God 'in spirit and in truth' is first and foremost a way of saying that we must worship God by means of Christ. In Him the reality has dawned and the shadows are being swept away (Hebrews 8:13). Christian worship is new covenant worship; it is gospel-inspired worship; it is Christ-centered worship; it is cross-focused worship." Worship is experiencing our highest joy in Christ and finding fulfillment in His all-sufficient grace expressed for us in the gospel.

Christ is now the focus and inspiration for all true worship: ". . . true worshipers will worship the Father in Spirit and truth, for they are the kind of worshipers the Father seeks. God is spirit, and his worshipers must worship in the Spirit and in truth" (John 4:23–24). God inspires our worship in two ways: by His Holy Spirit and by His truth. God is Spirit, and because He created us in His image, every person is essentially a spiritual being. To worship God in an acceptable way requires your spirit to be made alive in Christ and joined to God: "Because of his great love for us, God . . . made us alive with Christ even when we were dead in transgressions" (Eph. 2:4–5; see also 1 Cor. 6:17). True worship is informed by God's truth, as revealed in the Bible, rather than one's imagination or religious traditions. Your response of worship must be according to the God revealed in the Scripture, and specifically in Christ.

The Living Sacrifice

The treasured Servant

From eternity past, God planned to sacrifice His Son, Jesus Christ, on the cross for our redemption: "Here is my servant, whom I uphold, my chosen one in whom I delight; I will put my Spirit on him, and he will bring justice to the nations" (Isa. 42:1). Consider the humility of Jesus as He describes His mission: "For even the Son of Man did not come to be served, but to serve, and to give his life as a ransom for many" (Mark 10:45). Christ served the Father by paying the debt for our sins and satisfying God's justice. He served us by dying in our place, as our substitute. In addition, He set the example for our lives by demonstrating how to serve others.

Considering all that Christ has done, you would think that God would require something from us in return. But Christ has done all that is required. "He is not served by human hands, as if he needed anything. Rather, he himself gives everyone life and breath and everything else. From one man he made all the nations, that they should inhabit the whole earth; and he marked out their appointed times in history and the boundaries of their lands. God did this so that they would seek him and perhaps reach out for him and find him, though he is not far from any one of us" (Acts 17:25–27). Worship is our response to the astounding work done by the Servant who, by His death, gave us life. Because of His service to the Father, we can rest: "There remains, then, a Sabbath-rest for the people of God; for anyone who enters God's rest also rests from his own work, just as God did from his. Let us, therefore, make every effort to enter that rest, so that no one will fall by following their example of disobedience" (Heb. 4:9–11).

As a young boy, I was enthralled with kite-flying. When I grew up enough to try it for myself, I soon discovered that the art of launching the kite into the air and sustaining its flight was quite a struggle. I tried repeatedly to throw the kite up in the air and then run as fast as my little legs would carry me. Yet, time after time the kite would quickly crash and drag behind me. I continued this same cycle, growing more discouraged with each attempt. Finally, a sympathetic friend offered his help. He explained how much easier it would be if I simply held up the kite in the air until lifted by the breeze. Once it was lifted by the wind, I would release more and more string and eventually the wind would lift the kite high into the sky. This new perspective

Worship is our response . . .

was the breakthrough I needed; my kite-flying career soon became legendary (in my own mind).

I learned something about my relationship with God from flying kites. Suppose the kite can think for itself, and it dreams about flying. However, if the kite hopes to fly, it cannot struggle against the wind; rather, it must yield to it. Once the kite recognizes the greatness of the wind and completely yields to it, flying is the natural result. In a similar way, worship is not something I struggle to do; it is simply recognizing the greatness of God and responding to Him. Once I yield to Him, worship is the natural overflow of my love. Christ lived the life we should have lived, and He died the death we should have died. He did all that was necessary to save us. Therefore, worship is recognizing the complete sufficiency of the gospel and resting from all self-salvation efforts. Worship is receiving the service Christ died to give you.

The reflected worth

We exist to magnify the greatness and sufficiency of Christ in all things: "I eagerly expect and hope that I will in no way be ashamed, but will have sufficient courage so that now as always Christ will be exalted in my body, whether by life or by death. For to me, to live is Christ and to die is gain" (Phil. 1:20–21). Worship is reflecting the worth and value of God. Through the gospel, we come to understand that nothing compares with the greatness of Christ, not even our own life.

Because of Christ, even death serves us because it liberates us into deeper intimacy with Christ. Worship is being happily satisfied with what God has done for you through Christ. "My grace is sufficient for you, for my power is made perfect in weakness" (2 Cor. 12:9). The apostle Paul described his satisfaction with Christ: "I have learned to be content whatever the circumstances. I know what it is to be in need, and I know what it is to have plenty. I have learned the secret of being content in any and every situation, whether well fed or hungry, whether living in plenty or in want. I can do all this through him who gives me strength" (Phil. 4:11–13). Cherishing Christ as greater than all that life can offer—family, career, retirement, fame, success, friends, or even wealth—enables you to be content in all circumstances. As John Piper[4] has said: "Christ is most glorified in us when we are most satisfied in him."

The expressed life

Worship is not confined to a specific time or place. Worship is to be your continuous response to His grace, expressed in every area of your life: "Therefore, I urge you, brothers and sisters, in view of God's mercy, to offer your bodies as a living sacrifice, holy and pleasing to God—this is your true and proper worship" (Rom. 12:1). There is no time when you are not to worship God. Worship is not limited to a weekly gathering with other believers, or even to your private devotional time with Him. Worship for God is to be expressed in all areas of life at all times. For example, you worship God by the way you do your work, how you relate to your friends, how you guard your heart from wrong thoughts, and how you freely forgive those who wrong you. Worship is wholeheartedly surrendering your life in response to His grace as an "offering." As author C. S. Lewis[5] has said, "We only learn to behave ourselves in the presence of God." Your entire and total self becomes an instrument of righteous worship: "Just as you used to offer the parts of your body in slavery to impurity and to ever-increasing wickedness, so now offer them in slavery to righteousness leading to holiness. When you were slaves to sin, you were free from the control of righteousness. What benefit did you reap at that time from the things you are now ashamed of? Those things result in death! But now that you have been set free from sin and have become slaves to God, the benefit you reap leads to holiness, and the result is eternal life" (Rom. 6:19–22). How you live your life expresses what you truly consider most valuable.

. . . what you truly consider most valuable.

The transformed life

Moses gazed into the glory of God as he spent forty days and nights on Mount Sinai. Afterward, when he returned to the camp, his face was shining and the people were afraid: "Moses was there with the Lord forty days and forty nights . . . he wrote on the tablets the words of the covenant—the Ten Commandments. When Moses came down from Mount Sinai . . . he was not aware that his face was radiant because he had spoken with the Lord . . . the people saw that his face was radiant" (Ex. 34:28–35). Moses reflected the glory of God after spending extended time gazing upon His beauty and holiness. As pastor Jack Hayford[6] says: "Worship changes the worshiper into the image of the One worshiped." As you focus your life on Christ, you will be transformed into His likeness. "We all, with unveiled face, beholding the glory of the Lord, are being transformed into the same image from one degree of glory to another. For this comes from the Lord who is the Spirit" (2 Cor. 3:18 ESV).

Authentic worship

Worship is active. Yet worship is not simply saying words or doing actions such as kneeling, praying, or singing. A person can do religious actions and yet his or her heart may be far from God. This type of "worship" is not true worship at all. God requires your worship to be wholehearted and pure: "These people honor me with their lips, but their hearts are far from me. They worship me in vain; their teachings are but rules taught by men" (Matt. 15:8–9; see also Isa. 29:13). Genuine worship must be a sincere expression of the heart. God longs for your affections for Him to come alive as you respond to the amazing truth of His magnificent love and grace. Authentic worship grieves over sin (Ps. 51) and longs for fellowship with God (Ps. 42:1–2). Heartfelt worship feels reverence and awe before the holiness and magnitude of God (Ps. 5:7). Sincere worship overflows with gratitude (Ps. 100:4), joy (Ps. 16:11), and intense love for God (Ps. 116:1–2). Prepare to express heartfelt worship to Jesus Christ through the projects listed next.

Projects and Practical Applications

1. Begin each day this week by finding a quiet place to meet with God. Follow the biblical practice of kneeling before the Lord, actually getting on your knees for prayer. Turn your thoughts to God's great love for you.

Wait for a moment in quietness, sensing His loving presence with you. Quote (or read) aloud the word in Eph. 2:4–5, "But because of his great love for us, God, who is rich in mercy, made us alive with Christ even when we were dead in transgressions—it is by grace you have been saved." Reflect on this truth, and be refreshed and strengthened by God's love and mercy for you. Then, personalize the verse and pray it out loud to Him in praise: "But because of Your great love for me, You who are rich in mercy, made me alive with Christ even when I was dead in transgressions. It is by grace I have been saved." Do this again and again until your heart is at rest in the work Christ has accomplished for you on the cross.

Why is it important to speak God's word out loud? Certainly silent and quiet prayers are legitimate expressions of worship. However, speaking God's word out loud will build your faith (Rom. 10:17) and strengthen your trust in Him.

2. Next, quote (or read) 1 John 1:9 as a prayer to the Lord. Once it is quoted, begin to confess to Him the sins He brings to your mind. Simply agree with Him about your sin, and confess your pride and unbelief in His goodness. Thank Him for His complete forgiveness and then gladly receive His cleansing. Next, personalize 1 John 1:9: "If I confess my sins, You are faithful and just and will forgive me my sins and purify me from all unrighteousness." Repeat it a few times to the Lord, until this truth frees you of all guilt. Treasure His forgiveness.

3. Finally, offer Him your life by quoting (or reading) Romans 12:1: "Therefore, I urge you, brothers and sisters, in view of God's mercy, to offer your bodies as a living sacrifice, holy and pleasing to God—this is your true and proper worship." Reflect again on God's mercy for you—expressed in the cross. He gave His life for you, so you can now give your life to Him. Next, personalize Romans 12:1 as a prayer: "Lord, in view of Your mercy for me, I offer my body to You as a living sacrifice, holy and pleasing to You as true and proper worship." Yield your life to Him—your motives, attitudes, thoughts, words, and actions. Present yourself to Him to be filled with His Spirit and sent forth to love all people He brings your way (your family, your coworkers, your neighbors, your friends, and all others). Dedicate all of your being to Him, and offer the day to Him to lead you however He chooses. Before you rise from your knees, wait to be filled with His love and joy. Be happy in Jesus before you leave the quiet place with Him.

Small group discussion:

1. Share with your group about your daily times of worship with the Lord. Where did you meet with Him? What was awkward for you? What brought peace or joy to your heart? Describe your awareness of God's presence.

2. Share your thoughts on why "the gospel is our fuel for worship."

3. How can your group pray and encourage you this week?

All Scripture is breathed out by God and profitable for teaching, for reproof, for correction, and for training in righteousness, that the man of God may be complete, equipped for every good work.

2 Tim. 3:16–17 ESV

Chapter Four

Scripture

SCRIPTURE

Among the most favorite memories from my childhood were the times my mother read Bible stories to me. I can still hear her gentle voice reading to me about God creating the world, Noah gathering all the animals in the ark, and Abraham and Sarah having a baby in their old age. I pictured in my mind how God used Moses to bring the plagues against Pharaoh and then miraculously led Israel out of Egypt. I was fascinated by the supernatural power God displayed for His people. Even though I did not understand every detail of the stories, I was aware that God was powerful, good, and loving toward His people.

. . . my mother read Bible stories to me.

When I was older, I was given a Bible, but since I was not yet a Christian, I did not have much interest in reading it for myself. The few times I did read it, I did not gain very much insight from it or understand much of its message. I think I was nervous that if God was real, I should surrender my life to Him. But my prideful independence did not want to submit to God, so it was a simple decision for me to ignore His message in the Bible.

Once I became a Christian, my attitude toward the Bible changed completely. Now I had a very strong interest in reading the Bible, and, surprisingly, I understood more and more of its message. I had particular interest in the life and teachings of Jesus as found in the first four books of the New Testament. The more I read, the stronger my faith grew, and the more meaningful my relationship with God became. The Bible became an essential resource in my journey with Jesus. Today, as a follower of Christ for many years, I have read through the Bible several times. Its message continues to inspire, strengthen, guide, and encourage me on a daily basis.

What is Scripture?

A supernatural collection of God's truth

The "Scriptures" are also called the "Bible" and "God's Word." Although the Bible looks like one book, it is actually a collection of sixty-six different books that are arranged like a library. In other words, just as books are grouped by type in a library (history, philosophy, decorating, auto repair, fiction, etc.), so are the books of the Bible. The main groups of the Bible include: the Law, history, wisdom, prophets, biography, theology, church issues and leadership, and the end times. The two main sections of the Bible are the Old Testament and the New Testament; the dividing line is the birth of Christ. The sixty-six books of the Bible were written over a fifteen-hundred-year span by over forty very different authors, including kings, fishermen, herdsmen, and farmers. The list also includes a prime minister, a medical doctor, a slave, a tax collector, and a Jewish rabbi—to name a few. The Bible was written on three continents (Asia, Europe, and Africa) and in three different languages (Hebrew, Aramaic, and Greek).

The story of God

The Bible is not written like a novel; nor are the books arranged chronologically. You cannot read it from front to back and expect the events to unfold in the order in which they occurred. However, in spite of this large time span over which it was written and the enormous cultural, economic, and geographical differences of its authors, there is an amazing unity in its message. The Bible is God's story. The Bible is the final authority from God. The authority of Scripture cannot be separated from the authority of God. Whatever the Bible affirms (or denies), it affirms (or denies) with the very authority of God.

What Does the Bible Say about Itself?

God communicates to us in the Bible

The Bible makes dramatic claims about its source and authority: "All Scripture is breathed out by God and profitable for teaching, for reproof, for correction, and for training in righteousness, that the man of God may be complete, equipped for every good work" (2 Tim. 3:16–17 ESV). The concept that Scripture is "breathed out by God" means it is a perfect expression of God's nature and thought. His Word represents Him and is infused with life. God's Word is profitable, for your life in every way. That is, His Word teaches you the way to live, reveals when you have left the way (reproof), makes clear how to align your life with God's way again (correction), and instructs how to remain in right fellowship with God (training in righteousness). God's Word is the critical resource for your spiritual development. The more experience you have believing and obeying God's Word in your life, the better equipped you are for every work of ministry.

His word represents Him . . .

God's Word is reliably from God

The apostle Peter was privileged to be with Jesus and learn from Him. Peter had the remarkable experience of hearing the audible voice of God when a voice from heaven affirmed Jesus as the Son of God (Matt. 17:5–6). Yet he writes in his letter that the written Scriptures are even more authoritative than the audible voice of God:

> We have something more sure, the prophetic word, to which you will do well to pay attention

> as to a lamp shining in a dark place, until the day dawns and the morning star rises in your hearts, knowing this first of all, that no prophecy of Scripture comes from someone's own interpretation. For no prophecy was ever produced by the will of man, but men spoke from God as they were carried along by the Holy Spirit (2 Peter 1:19–21 ESV).

. . . the written record of God's revelation . . .

"Hearing" God's voice can be very subjective; however, the written record of God's revelation is a certainty. What we think we hear from God in our hearts must always align with what God has already said in the Bible.

God supernaturally inspired the writings of the Bible. Though written by human authors, they were carried along to write exactly what the Holy Spirit wanted recorded. When men wrote the Scriptures, their statements did not originate in their own thinking but were put into their minds by the direct action of the Holy Spirit. They wrote the Word of God in the sense that they wrote words that came directly from God. God used their individual personalities (and even their writing styles), yet they composed and recorded without error His revelation to man. It is truly the Word God has spoken (1 Thess. 2:13).

How God's Word Impacts Your Life

God's Word reveals Jesus Christ

Before the universe was created, God is. He has always existed. It is difficult with human language to express God's eternal nature, but the apostle John wrote it as well as it can be written: "In the beginning was the Word, and the Word was with God, and the Word was God . . . And the Word became flesh and dwelt among us . . ." (John 1:1, 14 ESV). The Son of God is the Word. He is the perfect communication, or "Word" of God, in every way. In order to fully communicate His nature, God covered Himself in humanity (Incarnation) and became a man. The Word of God is Jesus, and Jesus is the Word of God. God reveals Himself in Christ as expressed in the Scriptures. If you want to know Christ, you will discover Him in the Bible.

God's Word gives spiritual life

The words Jesus spoke and the words of the Bible are not simply helpful ideas, inspirational phrases, and insightful concepts. The words of the Bible are life-giving. As Jesus said, "The Spirit gives life; the flesh counts for nothing. The words I have spoken to you are spirit and they are life" (John 6:63). True life (Greek: "zoe") is the life that emanates from God Himself. He is Life itself, and when His Word is welcomed into your heart, you experience His quality of life.

God's Word turns you from sin

The Bible has supernatural power to turn you away from sin and toward trusting God: "For the word of God is living and active. Sharper than any double-edged sword, it penetrates even to dividing soul and spirit, joints and marrow; it judges the thoughts and attitudes of the heart" (Heb. 4:12). The Bible evaluates and clarifies where my life is not aligned with God's will. It corrects and directs me to Him. It is not that I simply read my Bible; it is that the Bible "reads" me, revealing my hard heart and selfish rebellion. It exposes the prideful attitudes of my heart that destroy intimacy with God. God's Word inspires me to respond to Him: "The law of the Lord is perfect, reviving the soul. The statutes of the Lord are trustworthy, making wise the simple" (Ps. 19:7). God's Word revives my spirit so that I can turn to God and begin to live faithfully in glad submission to Him.

God's Word transforms and renews your mind

The Bible has a cleansing effect upon your mind and thoughts. It helps you learn to think as God thinks: "Do not conform any longer to the pattern of this world, but be transformed by the renewing of your mind. Then you will be able to test and approve what God's will is—his good, pleasing and perfect will" (Rom. 12:2). God's Word reveals God's will. As you trust and obey God's Word, you lose your attachment to the godless ways of this world. You begin to see the superior wisdom of God's way of life and adjust yourself to it. The more you believe and act upon God's Word, the more your decisions and attitudes will reflect God's wisdom (James 3:17). In this way, God's Word transforms your mind.

God's Word counsels and guides

. . . the richest resource of wisdom . . .

Apart from God, you cannot know what is ultimately best for your life. God reveals His guidance to you in the Scriptures: "Your word is a lamp to my feet and a light for my path" (Ps. 119:105). Though the Scriptures do not address every detail of life, they do speak to all the major issues of life. The Bible provides the richest resource of wisdom, counsel, and guidance a person could ever need. When you bring your problems and questions to the Scriptures, God will reveal His counsel to you and guide you to what is best.

God's Word generates faith

Many times Jesus would tell someone requesting healing to "believe" Him. When they heard His Word, faith was generated in their heart, and their faith brought God's power (Mark 10:52). The Scriptures have supernatural power to produce faith in those who hear them: "Faith comes from hearing, and hearing through the word of Christ" (Rom. 10:17 ESV). This is why we benefit by reading, studying, meditating, speaking, praying, and acting upon God's Word—it strengthens our faith. Your confidence in God grows the more you hear, believe, and act upon the Scriptures.

"... my joy may be in you ..."

God's Word gives hope

Hope is rooted in the goodness of God. Hope is the certainty that God is in control of all things and that He can be trusted to do what is ultimately for my good. Reading and reflecting on the "case studies" of how God provided for Israel gives you hope that He will do the same for you: "Everything that was written in the past (Old Testament) was written to teach us, so that through endurance and the encouragement of the Scriptures we might have hope" (Rom. 15:4).

God's Word is the true source of joy

Jesus said, "These things I have spoken to you that my joy may be in you, and that your joy may be full" (John 15:11 ESV). There is no greater joy than to live in the constant awareness of God's love, acceptance, and grace. As God's Word becomes your meditation, you will enjoy rich communion with Him and experience His joy (Ps. 16:11).

God's Word sanctifies

Jesus prayed for His disciples that God's Word would be at work in their lives: "Sanctify them by the truth; your word is truth" (John 17:17). "Sanctify" means that God sets you apart as His special possession and for His exclusive use. God's Word has an amazing ability to separate you from that which is evil and unite you with God's holiness. His Word creates a new love for Him and a desire to respond to Him more completely.

God's Word nourishes

Jesus responded to the temptation to doubt God's goodness by quoting Deuteronomy 8:3, "Man does not live on bread alone, but on every word that comes from the mouth of God" (Matt. 4:4). Everyone knows the importance of eating food to sustain life. Jesus says that the spiritual food of God's Word is even more vital than natural food. God's Word is the spiritual nutrition that alone can nourish your soul.

God's Word purifies

Reading and meditating on God's Word leads you to think God's thoughts and cleanses your mind of mental garbage: "Whatever is true, whatever is honorable, whatever is just, whatever is pure, whatever is lovely, whatever is commendable, if there is any excellence, if there is anything worthy of praise, think about these things" (Phil. 4:8 ESV). Peter tells his fellow believers, "I have written both of them (letters we now have in our New Testament) as reminders to stimulate you to wholesome thinking" (2 Peter 3:1).

God's Word empowers

Whatever God says is true and reliable. When you trust what God has said, you are empowered to live in spiritual victory: "He has given us his very great and precious promises, so that through them you may participate in the divine nature and escape the corruption in the world caused by evil desires" (2 Peter 1:4). God's Word is filled with promises He has made and intends to keep (2 Cor. 1:20). When you believe these promises and persevere in faith, God fulfills His promise and empowers you to live supernaturally (Rom. 4:20–21; Heb. 6:12).

God's Word brings freedom

Jesus taught His disciples that knowing and obeying His truth is the only way to lasting freedom: "If you hold to my teaching, you are really my disciples. Then you will know the truth, and the truth will set you free" (John 8:31–32). God's Word is absolute truth, revealing the way God intends for us to live. When you believe and apply His Word in your life, you experience freedom from the bondage of sin. There is no other possibility for true, inner freedom: "I run in the path of your commands, for you have set my heart free" (Ps. 119:32).

God's Word gives lasting peace

God's Word is intended not simply to fill your mind, but to be at home in your heart: "Let the peace of Christ rule in your hearts" . . . and "let the word of Christ dwell in you richly" (Col. 3:15–16). When I regularly receive God's Word into my heart, His peace saturates my life. Peace is the certainty that God has provided everything I need for my well-being and happiness. When you dwell on God's Word, you trust Christ to be all you need, and the result is peace.

. . . His peace saturates my life.

What is God's Word Like?

Seed

"The sower sows the word . . . those that were sown on the good soil are the ones who hear the word and accept it and bear fruit" (Mark 4:14, 20 ESV).

Food

"When your words came, I ate them; they were my joy and my heart's delight" (Jer. 15:16).

Milk

"Like newborn babies, crave pure spiritual milk, so that by it you may grow up in your salvation, now that you have tasted that the Lord is good" (1 Peter 2:2–3).

Honey

"They (God's commands) are sweeter than honey, than honey from the honeycomb" (Ps. 19:10).

Light

"Your word is a lamp to my feet and a light for my path" (Ps. 119:105).

Sword

"Take the sword of the Spirit, which is the word of God" (Eph. 6:17). "For the word of God is living and active. Sharper than any double-edged sword, it penetrates even to dividing soul and spirit, joints and marrow; it judges the thoughts and attitudes of the heart" (Heb. 4:12).

Fire

"His word is in my heart like a fire, a fire shut up in my bones. I am weary of holding it in; indeed, I cannot" (Jer. 20:9).

Hammer

"Is not my word like fire," declares the LORD, "and like a hammer that breaks a rock in pieces?" (Jer. 23:29).

Water

"Christ loved the church and gave himself up for her to make her holy, cleansing her by the washing with water through the word" (Eph. 5:25–26).

Breath

"All Scripture is God-breathed . . ." (2 Tim 3:16).

Daily bread from heaven

Israel's physical hunger for daily food became an instrument God used to teach faith. God provided daily food for the people called "manna" (Ex. 16:31). God caused this "bread from heaven" (Ex. 16:4) to appear each morning (Ex. 16:13–16). The people were to gather each day enough manna for their needs. However, if they kept some overnight, it would spoil and be useless by the next morning (Ex. 16:20). The manna from yesterday would not nourish today. God gave manna not only for their nourishment but also to prove His trustworthiness to care for them and to provide all they needed. "He humbled you, causing you to hunger and then feeding you with manna . . . to teach you that man does not live on bread alone but on every word that comes from the mouth of the Lord" (Deut. 8:3).

Later, Jesus referenced this historical experience as He proclaimed: "It is not Moses who has given you the bread from heaven, but it is my Father who gives you the true bread from heaven. For the bread of God is he who comes down from heaven and gives life to the world . . . I am the bread of life. He who comes to me will never go hungry, and he who believes in me will never be thirsty"

"bread from heaven"

God desires to meet with you . . .

(John 6:32–35). Jesus wants you to feed daily on His Word. He wants to nourish your soul with the gospel. He wants His followers to learn to trust His Word as their daily spiritual food.

Experiencing the Power of God's Word

Prepare to meet personally with God

Meeting alone with God is not like going to school or sitting in a classroom simply to learn information. God desires to meet with you "in person," in the context of a very loving and intimate relationship. He calls you to come and meet with Him to enjoy His fellowship (1 John 1:3). Jesus invited His disciples to rest from the work of ministry in order to refresh their relationship with Him: "Then, because so many people were coming and going that they did not even have a chance to eat, he said to them, 'Come with me by yourselves to a quiet place and get some rest'" (Mark 6:31). Meeting with Jesus should be like having a meaningful conversation with a trusted counselor and mentor. You meet with God already knowing you are loved, accepted, and forgiven. Meeting with Christ is to be with your best Friend who loves you perfectly and is your wisest Counselor:

"I will ask the Father, and he will give you another Counselor to be with you forever—the Spirit of truth

. . . you know him, for he lives with you and will be in you . . . the Counselor, the Holy Spirit, whom the Father will send in my name, will teach you all things and will remind you of everything I have said to you" (John 14:16–17, 26).

Meeting daily with God in the Scriptures is not only to gain knowledge, but also to experience the living Christ: "You diligently study the Scriptures because you think that by them you possess eternal life. These are the Scriptures that testify about me" (John 5:39; see also Luke 24:32, 45).

Set an appointment to meet with God every day

It is important to establish your time with God as a daily appointment and consistently keep it. Meeting with God in the morning seems to be His recommendation (Ex. 16:21; Lev. 6:12). "In the morning, O Lord, you hear my voice; in the morning I lay my requests before you and wait in expectation" (Ps. 5:3). Meeting with God in the Scriptures should be your daily habit: "The Bereans . . . with great eagerness . . . examined the Scriptures every day" (Acts 17:11). Determine when and where you will meet with God. It should be a place where you can learn from Him without distraction: "Very early in the morning, while it was still dark, Jesus got up, left the house and went off to a solitary place, where he prayed" (Mark 1:35). Also, it is very helpful to have a Bible reading plan. Without a plan, your reading will be aimless and can be confusing. There are numerous possibilities: reading through the New Testament in one year, or reading through the entire Bible in one year, or you can find several online options at *www.bible.com*

Come to God's Word with a seeking heart

God wants you to discover the wisdom, encouragement, and power of His word that will address the daily concerns of your heart. Like a father counseling His child, God invites you to eagerly search His Word for the answers and solutions you need for your daily problems: "If you look for it as for silver and search for it as for hidden treasure, then you will understand the fear of the Lord and find the knowledge of God" (Prov. 2:4–5). Consider the areas of your life that often burden you: worries about relationships, family conflicts, financial pressures, health needs, and career issues. Bring these specific concerns to God's Word each day and expect God to highlight particular Bible verses in your daily reading that will address your needs. In this way, you are searching for God's treasures of wisdom in your daily Scripture reading. You will be surprised how frequently God will "speak" to you in the Scriptures in a way that ignites your faith. When we hear with our spiritual ears the Word of God that specifically speaks to

When we hear with our spiritual ears . . . our faith is strengthened.

the needs in our lives, our faith is strengthened: "Faith comes from hearing, and hearing through the word of Christ" (Rom. 10:17 ESV). The "word of Christ" is *rhema,* which refers to the "spoken" Word of God. As you read the written word of God, the living voice of God will speak to your heart from the Scriptures. In your daily time in God's Word, expect to hear His voice speaking to you a specific Scripture verse to be your special treasure.

Learn the skills of Bible study

Studying the Bible requires learning new skills. These skills are like tools for a builder—the more you practice, the better you become: "Do your best to present yourself to God as one approved, a workman who does not need to be ashamed and who correctly handles the word of truth" (2 Tim. 2:15). The best way to study the Bible is with the "inductive" method of study. It means letting the Bible speak for itself (by observing, interpreting, and applying the text), rather than bringing your own presupposition to the text. This type of study helps prevent misinterpretation of the Bible's teachings. You do not need to utilize every question listed below for every Bible verse. The idea is to read it with the right perspective. With practice, you will improve your ability to understand God's Word:

Observation: **What does it say?**

Where did this take place?

When did it take place?

Who was involved?

What happened?

What ideas are expressed?

What are the significant words or phrases?

What are the results?

Interpretation: **What does it mean?**

What did it mean to the original audience?

What is the main idea?

Why did it happen?

How does this passage relate to the rest of the chapter and book?

What other Scripture passages relate to this passage?

Application: **What do I need to do**?

Is there a principle to learn?

Is there an example to follow?

Is there a sin to avoid?

Is there a promise to claim?

Is there a command to obey?

Is there a challenge to face?

Is there an attitude to adjust?

What do I need to do, and when?

What do I sense God saying to me today?

Encourage others with what you have heard from God

What you learn from God's Word and in fellowship with Him is not only for your benefit but also for the benefit of others. Make it your goal each day to share what you learn with at least one person from your family, your friends, your coworkers, and your brothers and sisters in Christ. "Let the word of Christ dwell in you richly as you teach and admonish one another with all wisdom" (Col. 3:16). Your humble comments of how the Lord taught you that day from the Scriptures will bring much encouragement to others: "Encourage one another daily . . . so that none of you may be hardened by sin's deceitfulness" (Heb. 3:13).

Make it your goal to be satisfied with Christ

George Mueller[7] was a nineteenth-century man of prayer and faith who established orphanages throughout England. He learned to depend on God alone to meet all the needs of his life and ministry. At age thirty-six, he discovered a vital truth: "My first great and primary business to which I ought to attend every day was to have my soul happy in the Lord, that my inner man might be nourished." What was Mueller's secret for a happy life in Christ?

For 10 years I had the habit of beginning my day with prayer. However, now I see that the most important thing I had to do was to give myself to the reading of the word of God and to meditation on it that my heart might be comforted, encouraged, warned and instructed. While meditating, my heart would be brought into communion with the Lord. I would search every verse to get the blessing out of it—not to preach it or teach it—but to obtain food for my own soul. Now I speak to my Father and my Friend about the things that he has brought before me in his precious word. Food for the inner man is not the simple reading of the word, so that it only passes through our minds, just as water runs thru a pipe, but considering what we read, pondering over it and applying it to our hearts. I dwell on this point because of the immense spiritual profit and refreshment I have derived from it myself after having done it for 40 years. How differently my day goes when the soul is refreshed and made happy early in the morning than without it once the service, the trials and temptations of the day come.

Projects and Practical Applications

1. Set an appointment to meet with God for at least fifteen minutes every day this week.

2. During your daily quiet time with the Lord, spend time reading the Scriptures and praying.

3. Humbly share what you gain from the Scriptures with someone at least once during the week.

Small group discussion:

1. Share with your group about your daily time with the Lord. How consistent were you? What was the greatest struggle? What was the greatest blessing?

2. Share one key insight from your Bible reading that was especially meaningful to you.

3. How can your group encourage you to continue meeting with the Lord for the next seven days?

Do not be anxious about anything, but in every situation, by prayer and petition, with thanksgiving, present your requests to God. And the peace of God, which transcends all understanding, will guard your hearts and your minds in Christ Jesus.

Phil. 4:6–7

Chapter Five

Prayer

PRAYER

Almost everyone has prayed at one time or another because there is just something in our hearts that tells us God exists and that He listens to our prayers. But, for some, it is only when facing a crisis that prayer is considered. I remember my first meaningful encounter with prayer. I was a teenager out with friends at a swimming party when a particular young man spoke rudely to me and mocked me. Feeling provoked and that my honor had been attacked, I replied in an equally rude and condescending way. Though my friends laughed at my comments, the other young man became furious and attacked me, beating me with his fists. At the time, I did not know he was a champion boxer and four years older than me, but I quickly discovered that I was no match for him. I found myself on the ground, being pummeled. Finally, others pulled him off of me. I scrambled to my feet, apologized to him for my comments, and ran home from the party bleeding, bruised, and embarrassed.

Almost everyone has prayed . . .

When I returned home, I washed my wounds, lay down on the floor of my bedroom, and replayed in my mind the entire terrible scene that led to my suffering. I deeply regretted the harsh words I had spoken. Strangely, my thoughts turned toward God, and I wondered if He saw what had happened and if He could protect me from this kind of trauma in the future. In that moment, at age fifteen, I prayed the most sincere prayer I had ever prayed in my life: "God, please protect me from any more fights; I promise never to provoke anyone again." In my heart, I felt God's comforting presence like never before, and it left me overwhelmed and in tears. Two years later, I became a Christian, but that simple prayer created a new level of authentic connection between God and me. I experienced a taste of the intimate relationship with God that is possible through prayer.

Prayer Defined

Prayer is communion

Prayer is communion with God—a supernatural, spiritual communication made possible by the finished work of Jesus Christ on the cross. Prayer is consciously responding to God's Spirit and God's truth; it is enjoying loving fellowship with Him. Prayer includes listening to God, being silent in the presence of God, crying to God, making requests to God, pouring out your heart to God, reflecting with God, discussing needs with God, questioning God, interceding to God, praising God, repenting to God, obeying God, and enjoying God. Prayer is the environment for closeness and intimacy with God that can occur anytime, anywhere, and is intended to be a continual experience for the follower of Christ.

Prayer Has Purpose

Prayer displays the victory of the gospel

Every time a believer prays, it reveals the grace of the gospel. Through the cross, Christ has opened the way to the Father. He has sacrificed His own blood, obtained our forgiveness, and now goes to the Father as priest on our behalf (Heb. 10:19–23). As believers, our prayers confirm that the work of Christ was sufficient to satisfy the justice of God, and we are welcomed as forgiven sinners into His presence. Even the simplest of prayers, offered in faith, declare with earth-shaking power the victory of Christ, who has opened the way to the Father.

Prayer glorifies God

When we ask and God answers, it makes known God's goodness and power. God delights to make His greatness known to a skeptical world by answering simple, humble prayers: "I will do whatever you ask in my name, so that the Son may bring glory in the Father. You may ask me for anything in my name, and I will do it" (John 14:13–14). Consider the powerful promise of Ephesians 3:20: God is "able to do immeasurably more than all we ask or imagine, according to his power that is at work within us." God values our prayers so much that He keeps them as His precious treasure: "Each one had a harp and they were holding golden bowls full of incense, which are the prayers of the saints" (Rev. 5:8). Oswald Chambers,[8] author of *My Utmost for His Highest,* wrote: "Prayer does not prepare us for a greater work, it is the greater work."

God values our prayers . . .

Prayer aligns you with God's purposes

Prayer does not change the mind of God; rather, true prayer changes the one praying. Prayer is the place where I move toward God as He reveals His plan for me. Even the most difficult assignments from God are welcomed into our hearts during prayer. In prayer, Jesus aligned Himself with the Father's will: "Father, if you are willing, take this cup from me; yet not my will, but yours be done" (Luke 22:42). Prayer provides the opportunity to trust God to accomplish His magnificent purposes. It is no surprise that Paul prayed for believers to know the hope and riches we have in Christ: "I pray also that the eyes of your heart may be enlightened in order that you may know the hope to which he has called you, the riches of his glorious inheritance in the saints" (Eph. 1:18). Prayer leader Dick Eastman[9] wrote, "Only those who see the invisible can attempt the impossible."

Prayer follows the example of Christ

Jesus made prayer a priority: "Very early in the morning, while it was still dark, Jesus got up, left the house and went off to a solitary place, where he prayed" (Mark 1:35). Even though there were still many needy people to care for, Jesus prioritized time with His Father: "He went up on a mountainside by himself to pray" (Matt. 14:23), and we read that "Jesus often withdrew to lonely places and prayed" (Luke 5:16). Christ considered prayer so important that the night before His crucifixion, when He would have had many concerns on His mind, He was praying for His disciples (John 17:6–19). British evangelist John Wesley[10] wrote, "God does nothing but by prayer, and everything with it."

Prayer develops intimacy with God

Jesus taught that the secret place of quiet prayer is the ideal environment for closeness with God: "When you pray, go into your room, close the door and pray to your Father, who is unseen. Then your Father, who sees what is done in secret, will reward you" (Matt. 6:6). The priority of the psalmist was an unhurried gaze into the riches of God's heart: "One thing I ask of the Lord, this is what I seek: that I may dwell in the house of the Lord all the days of my life, to gaze upon the beauty of the Lord and to seek him in his

"... pray to your Father, who is unseen."

temple" (Ps. 27:4). Eighteenth-century pastor and president of Princeton University Jonathan Edwards[11] wrote, "Prayer is to be as natural an expression of faith as breathing is to life." The habit of extended prayer is the way a person grows close and comfortable in God's presence.

Prayer brings God's wisdom and guidance

God is the wisest Being in the universe, so His plan for your life is exactly what you would choose for yourself if you had all the facts. One way a person gains God's perspective and wisdom is through prayer: "If any of you lacks wisdom, he should ask God, who gives generously to all . . ." (James 1:5). God will guide you by answering your prayers: "How gracious he will be when you cry for help! As soon as he hears, he will answer you . . . Whether you turn to the right or to the left, your ears will hear a voice behind you, saying, 'This is the way; walk in it'" (Isa. 30:19–21). He is eager to share His wisdom with those who are willing to ask: "Call to me and I will answer you and tell you great and unsearchable things you do not know" (Jer. 33:3). British author Richard Trench[12] wrote: "Prayer is not getting man's will done in heaven, but getting God's will done on earth. It is not overcoming God's reluctance but laying hold of God's willingness."

It is clear from the Scriptures that God intends for you to know His will, and then to guide you into it. He guides us by answering our prayers. Paul needed guidance for his missionary travels: "I pray that now at last by God's will the way may be opened for me to come to you" (Rom. 1:10). Knowing the importance of having God's guidance, he wrote to the church at Colosse, " . . . from the day we heard, we have not ceased to pray for you, asking that you may be filled with the knowledge of his will in all spiritual wisdom and understanding" (Col. 1:9 ESV). John Wesley[13] depended upon God's guidance so much that he wrote, "I have so much to do that I must pray several hours before I'm able to do it."

Prayer helps you depend on God

On the night He was to be arrested and later crucified, Jesus agonized in prayer: "'Father,' he said, 'everything is possible for you. Take this cup from me. Yet not what I will, but what you will'" (Mark 14:36). Prayer is the place where we learn best to depend upon God's gracious sovereignty. This is especially true when going through severe trials and feeling disoriented in prayer. God knows your need and will lead you in prayer by His Spirit (Rom. 8:26–27).

Prayer brings joy

Spending time with your loving, heavenly Father will bring joy to your heart. This joy is amplified when you experience precise answers to specific prayers: "My

Father will give you whatever you ask in my name . . . Ask and you will receive, and your joy will be complete" (John 16:23–24). This is why joyful prayer is to be the atmosphere in which we live: "Be joyful always, pray continually, give thanks in all circumstances; for this is God's will for you in Christ Jesus" (1 Thess. 5:16–18).

Prayer develops strong faith

"Ask and you will receive, and your joy will be complete."

"If anyone says to this mountain, 'Go, throw yourself into the sea,' and does not doubt in his heart but believes that what he says will happen, it will be done for him. Therefore I tell you, whatever you ask for in prayer, believe that you have received it, and it will be yours" (Mark 11:23–24). One of the greatest champions of prayer was George Mueller,[14] as previously mentioned, a pastor and founder of several orphanages and schools. Throughout his lifetime, he prayed and received dramatic answers for financial support and other provisions for thousands of orphans. He wrote, "Patient, persevering, believing prayer offered up to God, in the name of the Lord Jesus, has always, sooner or later, brought the blessing." Persevering in prayer develops your faith in God's perfect timing for His answers: "Jesus told his disciples . . . that they should always pray and not give up" (Luke 18:1). We are to "imitate those who through faith and patience inherit what has been promised" (Heb. 6:12). God responds to our confidence in Him to answer: "If you believe, you will receive whatever you ask for in prayer" (Matt. 21:22).

Prayer brings God's answers

God delights to answer prayer: "Before they call I will answer; while they are still speaking I will hear" (Isa. 65:24). God brings needs into our lives to drive us to pray: "I sought the Lord, and he answered me; he delivered me from all my fears" (Ps. 34:4). The needs for which we pray lead us to seek Him, which in turn, causes God to answer, proving His goodness: "Ask and it will be given to you; seek and you will find; knock and the door will be opened to you. For everyone who asks receives; he who seeks finds; and to him who knocks, the door will be opened" (Matt. 7:7–8). We can confidently ask God for what we need because He is a loving Father who listens when we cry out to Him (1 John 5:14–15). Inner-city missionary F. B. Meyer[15] wrote: "The greatest tragedy of life is not unanswered prayer, but unoffered prayer."

God delights to answer prayer.

Prayer brings God's provision

God lacks nothing and possesses all the resources you will ever need. He gladly gives you everything you need in answer to prayer: "Let us then approach the throne of grace with confidence, so that we may receive mercy and find grace to help us in our time of need" (Heb. 4:16). A lack of prayer leads to a lack of provision: "You do not have because you do not ask God" (James 4:2). God will meet your needs in direct answer to prayer: "The prayer of a righteous man is powerful and effective" (James 5:16).

Prayer conquers stress and worry

Prayer is the perfect antidote to worry: "Do not be anxious about anything, but in everything, by prayer and petition, with thanksgiving, present your requests to God. And the peace of God, which transcends all understanding, will guard your hearts and your minds in Christ Jesus" (Phil. 4:6–7). You can either worry or you can pray in faith—but you cannot do both at the same time. God intends for you to "Cast all your anxiety on him because he cares for you" (1 Peter 5:7). The smaller your faith, the greater your worries; the greater your faith, the smaller your worries. Puritan pastor Richard Alleine[16] wrote: "The reason why we obtain no more in prayer is because we expect no more. God usually answers us according to our own hearts." Praying in faith liberates you from the burden of stress and worry.

Prayer gives victory over temptation

Jesus taught Simon Peter the link between prayer and victory over Satan's temptations: "Simon, Simon, Satan has asked to sift all of you as wheat. But I have prayed for you, Simon, that your faith may not fail. And when you have turned back, strengthen your brothers" (Luke 22:31–33). The stronger your prayer life, the greater the victory you have in Christ over temptation. Jesus told His disciples: "Watch and pray so that you will not fall into temptation. The spirit is willing, but the body is weak" (Matt. 26:41). The devil will provide every conceivable distraction to prayer because he knows its power. British pastor Guy H. King[17] wrote, "No one is a firmer believer in the power of prayer than the devil; not that he practices it, but he suffers from it."

Prayer unites all believers

Prayer has always been part of the Christ-honoring church. It characterized the first church in Jerusalem as evidenced by the outpouring of the Spirit as the believers "devoted themselves to . . . prayer" (Acts 2:42) and "raised their voices together in prayer to God . . ." (Acts 4:24). The Antioch church was a praying church and became the greatest missionary church of the first century: "After they had fasted and prayed, they placed their hands on them (Saul and Barnabas) and sent them off (on a church-planting journey)" (Acts 13:3). There is nothing quite like prayer to bring unity among people. Jesus gave an inspiring promise that should motivate unity in prayer: "If two of you on earth agree about anything you ask for, it will be done for you by my Father in heaven. For where two or three come together in my name, there am I with them" (Matt. 18:19–20). Honest prayer causes you to evaluate your own attitudes toward others: "And when you stand praying, if you hold anything against anyone, forgive them, so that your Father in heaven may forgive you your sins" (Mark 11:25). Prayer for others also increases your love for them: "I thank my God every time I remember you. In all my prayers for all of you, I always pray with joy" (Phil. 1:3–4).

Prayer extends the influence of the gospel

Prayer for others also increases your love for them.

Prayer and evangelism go hand in hand. Paul repeatedly requested prayer for his outreach: "Pray also for me, that whenever I open my mouth, words may be given me so that I will fearlessly make known the mystery of the gospel" (Eph. 6:19); "Pray for us, too, that God may open a door for our message, so that we may proclaim the mystery of Christ" (Col. 4:3); "Brothers and sisters, pray for us that the message of the Lord may spread rapidly and be honored, just as it was with you" (2 Thess. 3:1). Evangelist D. L. Moody[18] wrote, "Every great movement of God can be traced to a kneeling figure."

Prayer Problems

French theologian and missionary Francois Fenelon[19] said, "Of all the activities of our faith in Christ, nothing is more essential or more neglected than prayer."

Boredom or disinterest

Prayer can become somewhat dull, as if you are talking to the wall rather than a person. What causes this problem? Possibly your prayers have become a monologue, rather than a dialogue, and you have grown tired of hearing your own voice as your mind wanders. Maybe you have no sense that God is listening or wanting to respond. Maybe you struggle to set aside time for prayer, but the truth is that we make time for the people we truly want to spend time with. Maybe prayer has become only a routine, and you have lost a passion to be with Him. Do you know that God not only listens, He speaks? He wants interaction: "The Counselor, the Holy Spirit, whom the Father will send in my name, will teach you all things and will remind you of everything I have said to you" (John 14:26). He initiated all that is good in your life: "Out of all the people on the face of the earth, the Lord has chosen you to be his treasured possession" (Deut. 14:2). Our response should be to find our greatest joy in Him: "Come near to God and he will come near to you" (James 4:8).

Guilt

Possibly your past failures have led to feelings of guilt. You avoid prayer because you feel you should produce a record of good behavior before approaching God. However, that wrong perception blinds you to the reality of God's nature—He forgives sin! Do not carry the burden of guilt; confess your sins to God and experience His gracious forgiveness: "God rescued us from dead-end alleys and dark dungeons. He set us up in the kingdom of the Son He loves so much, the Son who got us out of the pit we were in, got rid of the sins we were doomed to keep repeating" (Col. 1:14, The Message).

Busyness

Does it seem you never have time for meaningful, unhurried prayer? Possibly your daily schedule is crowded with good and necessary activities that interfere with your fellowship with God. If so, rethink your priorities and time management: ". . . understand the present time. The hour has come for you to wake up from your slumber, because our salvation is nearer now than when we first believed. The night is nearly over; the day is almost here. So let us put aside the deeds of darkness and put on the armor of light" (Rom. 13:11–12). If you are too busy for regular appointments with God, you are busier than He intends for you to be.

Unbelief

A chief enemy of prayer is a lack of faith: you do not truly believe God is going to do anything about your request. Possibly you have learned "not to expect too much from God" because in the past you have been disappointed over (perceived) unanswered prayer. Perhaps your prayers are so generalized that you would not even know if God did answer. Prayer should not be a dutiful obligation but rather a confident trust that God will take care of your needs: "You may ask me for anything in my name, and I will do it" (John 14:14).

Self-righteous attitude

If we approach God on the basis of personal goodness, we will never experience true grace or intimacy with Him (Titus 3:4–7). Consider the story Jesus told in Luke 18:9–14 involving the prayers of an arrogant Pharisee and a humble tax collector. It is no surprise that Jesus affirmed the one who honestly acknowledged his need for God's mercy.

Selfish motives

If your prayers sound more like a shopping list for God, you have missed the true purpose of prayer. Prayer is not about coercing God into getting your way. Prayer is aligning your heart with God's plan and staying consistent with His purposes: "You do not have because you do not ask God. When you ask, you do not receive, because you ask with wrong motives, that you may spend what you get on your pleasures" (James 4:2–3).

Performance

Prayer is not a stage where you perform to impress God and others. Jesus rebuked this kind of hypocrisy: "And when you pray,

Prayer is not about coercing God into getting your way.

do not be like the hypocrites, for they love to pray standing in the synagogues and on the street corners to be seen by men. I tell you the truth, they have received their reward in full" (Matt. 6:5). Hypocritical prayers like these are not even about God; they are using God to gain status with people. Also, some people feel God expects them to use religious words or special phrases in prayer. Rather than speaking simply and honestly, they use terms or a tone of voice in prayer that they never use when talking with friends. This should not be so. True prayer is to be vulnerable with God, not hiding behind religious wording. The more authentic you can be in prayer, the better your relationship with God will become. South African pastor Andrew Murray[20] wrote: "Some people pray just to pray, and some people pray to know God."

Developing a Powerful Life of Prayer

Find a special place for prayer

Jesus taught that a quiet and private place is the best environment to meet alone with God: "But when you pray, go into your room, close the door and pray to your Father, who is unseen" (Matt. 6:6). Determine a place where you can meet with God your Father without distractions. The place you choose should be as free from distractions as possible. If thoughts about other responsibilities distract you, simply make a note as they come to mind and turn your attention back to God; He is eager to meet with you. As soon as you close the door, your Father is there for you.

Present yourself honestly to God

The disciples needed to be taught how to pray because it was not something they automatically knew. One of the first critical lessons on prayer that Jesus taught them was to simply be themselves with no pretense: "When you pray, do not keep on babbling like pagans, for they think they will be heard because of their many words. Do not be like them, for your Father knows what you need before you ask him" (Matt. 6:7–9). God is not impressed with formal, religious prayers. There is nothing you can hide from God; He knows your spiritual condition with perfect precision. Do not pretend to be hyper-spiritual in prayer; simply come honestly to Him. Prayer is conversation with God, so use the same types of words and tones with Him as you do with others. The length of the prayer is not crucial—extensive prayers do not move God any more than brief prayers do. What matters most is the faith and honesty in the prayer. Remember, you are sharing with your loving Father who knows your needs. He longs to hear you tell Him what is on your heart. Before Jesus came, it was inconceivable that God could be known personally as "Father." But Christ came to welcome all spiritual orphans into a new relationship with their true heavenly Father. True prayer begins with entering into a personal communion with our infinitely loving, patient, and caring heavenly Father. Sociology professor Dallas Willard[21] comments on prayer: "Kingdom praying and its effectiveness is entirely a matter of your heart being totally open and honest before God. It is a matter of what we are saying with our whole being, moving with resolute intent and clarity of mind in the flow of God's action. In apprenticeship to Jesus, this is one of the most important things we learn how to do. He teaches us how to be in prayer what we are in life and how to be in life what we are in prayer."

"... totally open and honest before God."

Follow a pattern (PRAY)

Jesus never taught His disciples how to preach, only how to pray. Knowing how to speak to God is more important than knowing how to speak to people. No one is a better teacher of prayer than Jesus: "This, then, is how you should pray . . ." (Matt. 6:9). To learn how to pray, simply pray. When it comes to prayer, practice makes perfect. This simple outline can help you establish a plan for prayer: PRAY.

P is for Praise

Matt. 6:9 "Our Father in heaven, hallowed be your name."

> *Recognize His loving readiness to meet with you.*

Begin your prayer by praising and thanking God for choosing you and saving you through the gospel. Recognize His loving readiness to meet with you; enjoy His presence. Prayer reminds you that life is not about you . . . it is about God. As your understanding of God's true nature grows, your enjoyment of prayer will grow because all prayer begins and ends with the Father.

Praise Him for saving you through the cross of Christ. It is always reassuring to begin prayer by quoting Eph. 2:4–5. When you praise Him for His saving grace you will be preaching the gospel to yourself! Also, learn to praise Him for His excellent character qualities. Praise Him for His wisdom, holiness, and grace. Praise Him for His forgiveness of your sins and His daily guidance for your life. Praise Him for His power at work in you, and for His sovereignty over all things. The more you learn of Him in His Word, the more substance will fill your praise to Him.

Matt. 6:10 "Your kingdom come, your will be done, on earth as it is in heaven."

Your praise to God will lead into the study of His Word. This is where the daily reading of God's Word intersects with your daily prayers. God's Word reveals God's kingdom "will" for your life. Our heavenly Father is also the King who rules the kingdom of heaven and intends to bring His perfect will from heaven to earth. The process that brings His will from heaven to earth is prayer.

R is for Repent

Matt. 6:12 "Forgive us our debts, as we also have forgiven our debtors . . ."

Time with God in prayer and His Word will reveal the hidden sin in your heart. This revelation is an expression of God's mercy, and it is His invitation to confess your sins to Him. Be sensitive to your proud attitudes, harsh words, unloving actions, and anything you have done to stain the reputation of Christ or offend others. Remember God's promise in 1 John 1:9; confess your specific sins to the Lord and turn from them. Receive His forgiveness and let Him free you of all guilt. Also, forgive everyone who has wronged or offended you. Forgive as you have been forgiven.

A is for Ask

Matt. 6:11 "Give us today our daily bread . . ."

Ask your Father for what you need each day. Nothing is too small to share with Him. Also, remember that true prayer is not trying to coerce God into doing what you want. You are not trying to compel an unwilling

God to listen. The Father knows what you need, but He waits for you to ask so that He can provide. He longs to give you everything you need. True prayer is yielding all we are to all we know of the Father's plan and then asking Him to fulfill it.

Y is for Yield

Matt. 6:13 "Lead us not into temptation, but deliver us from the evil one . . ."

Wholeheartedly surrender to God's loving leadership in your life. Recognize that there is nothing that can touch your life apart from His loving hand. Prepare to avoid tempting situations and to live boldly in the will of God. Even when your appointment with God ends, your ongoing fellowship with God does not. All of life is to be shared with God. Praying Rom. 12:1 is a helpful way to offer your life to Him. Your daily life is a partnership with Him to serve others in His love. When you leave your prayer closet, you enter the mission field. Invite the Spirit of Christ to live His life in and through you each day.

Projects and Practical Applications

1. Establish a daily appointment to meet with God. Choose a place that is quiet where you will not be interrupted or distracted. Set aside at least fifteen minutes to be with Him to read the Scriptures and pray. Many people choose to get up early in the morning, before others are awake, to have a quiet place at home to meet with God.

2. When you meet with God, simply follow the plan for prayer (PRAY) as outlined above. Take your time and pray slowly, talking to God honestly from your heart. Be listening for the impressions His Spirit may give you. Write down what you sense He may be leading you to know or do. Take time in the Scriptures and expect the Lord to impress a particular truth from the Bible. Write it down and ask the Lord to make clear what He wants you to know and do with His truth.

3. Do not be in a hurry; take time to enjoy God's presence and soak in His perfect love for you. Allow your heart to be filled with His Spirit and joy. Your pleasure will be found not in the mechanics of spiritual disciplines but in encountering Christ, your living Savior. Anticipate the many moments throughout the day that you will have to commune with Him and to be renewed in His love.

Small group discussion:

1. Share with your small group about your experiences in prayer. How consistent were you? What was your greatest struggle? What was your greatest encouragement?

2. Share one key insight from your Bible reading that was especially meaningful to you.

3. How can your group encourage you to continue meeting with the Lord for the next seven days?

When you fast, do not look somber as the hypocrites do, for they disfigure their faces to show men they are fasting. Truly I tell you, they have received their reward in full. But when you fast, put oil on your head and wash your face, so that it will not be obvious to men that you are fasting, but only to your Father, who is unseen; and your Father, who sees what is done in secret, will reward you.

Matt. 6:16–18

6

Chapter Six

Fasting

FASTING

I love to eat. There is a long list of foods I enjoy: Italian pasta, German bratwurst, Sichuan spicy fish soup, Mexican enchiladas, Thai fried noodles, American steaks, Shanghainese dumplings or Indian curries—the list is endless. Plus, I absolutely love fruits, vegetables, and desserts. I follow the philosophy, "eat first, talk later." My mother always cooked delicious food for our family, and I never missed a meal if at all possible. As an adult, eating became like a hobby of special interest to me.

The thought of intentionally missing a meal seemed like a bad idea.

When I became a Christian and heard about fasting, I was intrigued but also apprehensive. The thought of intentionally missing a meal seemed like a bad idea. I thought, "Why would God provide good food to eat, and then ask you not to eat it?" But, I eventually tried fasting. I began the first day of my first fast with the best of intentions, but, just like I feared, I got hungry. To make matters worse, I had not even skipped a meal yet! As the day continued, my mind wandered far from God; it seemed like the only thing I could think about was food. Every type of food seemed appetizing to me, even foods I never liked before. To complicate the situation, I developed a headache and felt weak. After work and back at home, I slowly passed by the refrigerator (which I knew was full of food), resentful that I was not allowed to open it and eat a snack. Before the night ended, I have to confess that I gave in to the temptation and devoured a bowl full of grapes. It was amazing to taste the delicious fruit again, but then I felt guilty that I had failed to sustain my first fast through even one day. I wondered if I had also failed God.

... eating food can become a substitute for fellowship with God.

Even though later in my journey with the Lord I was able to fast more successfully, I had questions: "Was fasting a work I must do to earn something from God?" I knew God created food for us to enjoy as well as to satisfy hunger. Yet, why was fasting something God encouraged His people to do? I came to understand that though food is an expression of God's grace toward us, eating food can become a substitute for fellowship with God. Sometimes we eat even though we are not hungry. I believe this is a misplaced solution to our soul-hunger for God. Fasting helps us to recover a hunger for fellowship with God, who alone ultimately satisfies our souls.

What Is Fasting?

Glorifying God

Biblical fasting is voluntarily abstaining from all or certain types of food and drink for purposes that glorify God. The methods may vary, but the underlying motivation is to make known the greatness of God. Fasting is referred to in the Old and New Testaments and before and after the resurrection of Christ. As Jesus taught, He said, "When you fast . . ." (Matt. 6:17), not if you fast, implying that His disciples would practice this spiritual discipline.

Responding to grace

For a believer, fasting is a genuine response to the grace of God expressed in the gospel. Your deep love for Christ leads to a loss of interest in food because a greater satisfaction in fellowship with Him has been found. Also, when the intensity of your love for Christ is fading away, fasting strives to recover what has been lost. John Piper[22] writes in *Hunger for God,* "Christian fasting, at its root, is the hunger of a home-sickness for God . . . Half of Christian fasting is that our physical appetite is lost because our homesickness for God is so intense. The other half is that our homesickness for God is threatened because our physical appetites are so intense." Fasting, therefore, can occur spontaneously from a heart in love with God, and fasting can be a discipline

It helps us rely less on food and more on God.

to restore a heart to love God. It helps us rely less on food and more on God.

Hungering for God

Fasting is not a contrived attempt to create a love for God. We love Him because He has first loved us. Our response to His grace should be one of longing for Him. Fasting is a way of saying sincerely with our whole body what are the true feelings of our hearts: "As the deer pants for streams of water, so my soul pants for you, O God. My soul thirsts for God, for the living God. When can I go and meet with God?" (Ps. 42:1–2).

Biblical examples of fasting

The Bible is filled with examples of fasting that show a great variety of purpose. Moses fasted for forty days and nights, seeking God's forgiveness for the rebellion of Israel (Deut. 9:9, 18). Hannah fasted and prayed that God would heal her infertility; God answered by giving her a son, Samuel (1 Sam. 1:5–11, 18–20). King David fasted to seek God's healing for his infant son (2 Sam. 12:15–16, 22–23). King Ahab fasted to seek God's forgiveness (1 Kings 21:27–29). King Jehoshaphat proclaimed a national fast seeking God's protection for Israel and victory on the battlefield (2 Chron. 20:3). The prophet Daniel fasted for three weeks in response to a vision of supernatural warfare (Dan. 10:3). The King of Nineveh proclaimed a fast, urgently seeking God's mercy from impending destruction (Jonah 3:5–10). In response to the recovery of God's Law, Nehemiah and Ezra led Israel to fast in repentance and reverence unto the Lord (Neh. 9:1–3). Ezra proclaimed a fast to seek God's protection for the journey of the remnant (Ezra 8:21–23). Queen Esther pleaded with her fellow Israelites to fast in order to escape annihilation under a new Persian law (Esther 4:16). An elderly prophetess, Anna, fasted regularly as an act of worship and devotion unto God (Luke 2:37). Jesus was led by the Spirit to fast in order to conquer Satan's temptations (Matt. 4:1–11). Saul fasted for three days and nights as he pondered the miraculous appearance of the Risen Christ who had spoken to him (Acts 9:9). The Antioch church fasted as they began new ministry and cross-cultural missions (Acts 13:3). Paul fasted to confirm God's choice of local church leadership (Acts 14:23).

Some fasts were only one day (1 Sam. 7:6; 2 Sam. 1:12; 2 Sam. 3:35; Judges 20:26). Some lasted three days (Esther 4:16; Acts 9:9, 17–19); others for a full week (1 Sam. 31:13; 2 Sam. 12:16–23). On rare occasions, a fast lasted two weeks (Acts 27:33–34), three weeks (Dan. 10:3–13), and even forty days (Ex. 24:18; Ex. 34:28; Matt. 4:2).

Wrong Reasons to Fast

Fasting to impress others

All people want to be praised by others, especially for their hard work and achievements. Few things are more gratifying to sinful hearts than being praised for religious accomplishments. This appetite influenced the religious leaders of Jesus' day, too. They loved the praise of men, but covered it with a pretense of love for God: "When you fast, do not look somber as the hypocrites do, for they disfigure their faces to show men they are fasting. I tell you the truth, they have received their reward in full" (Matt. 6:16). Their actions portrayed a heart for God, but their true motive was a desperate hope to be admired and approved by other people. They were fasting to be seen and praised by people rather than God. The kind of fasting Jesus advocates expresses worship unto the Lord as if He is the only One who will see. Fasting is not to impress others with our discipline or even to influence others to greater devotion. True fasting is coming to God in weakness, expressing our need in meekness, and longing for Him to become the greatest joy of our lives.

Fasting in self-righteousness

Fasting itself is of no spiritual value.

Fasting itself is of no spiritual value (Isa. 58:3–10; Jer. 14:12). It is to be an expression of faith in response to the gospel. Jesus told a story of a Pharisee who fasted twice a week and felt himself superior to less devoted worshippers. He believed God would answer his prayer because of his devotion. However, his fasting was only an expression of his self-righteousness and God was not impressed (Luke 18:12–14). Paul warned Timothy that false teachers would infiltrate the church and mislead believers into legalism by "order(ing) them to abstain from certain foods, which God created to be received with thanksgiving by those who believe and who know the truth" (1 Tim. 4:3). Legalism is the notion that a person can do certain actions in order to gain God's approval, to earn salvation. It is entirely possible to use fasting as an expression of self-righteousness. Paul warned that regulations to abstain from food may "have an appearance of wisdom, with their self-imposed worship, their false humility and their harsh treatment of the body, but they lack any value in restraining sensual indulgence" (Col. 2:23). Though others may be impressed by one's self-denial, God knows the heart. Fasting does not verify genuine faith or "restrain sensual indulgence." Fasting is not intended to be "willpower religion."

Fasting to manipulate God

Fasting is not a formula to obtain whatever you want from God. The people of Israel practiced the discipline of fasting and expected God would respond to their "work" by giving them what they requested. Yet their fasting was only a superficial exercise; they continued in selfishness, exploitation, and divisiveness. The prophet Isaiah revealed that God wanted their fasting to result in a change of heart, earnest humility, and sincere love for others (Isa. 58:3–10). King David had committed adultery with Bathsheba, and then he arranged for her husband's murder. The resulting pregnancy brought forth a baby boy born in sickness. David fasted, hoping God would be merciful and spare the infant's life; but no healing came (2 Sam. 12:22–23).

Right Reasons to Fast

Fasting for spiritual victory

As Jesus prepared to begin His public ministry, He was "led by the Spirit into the desert, where for forty days he was tempted by the devil. He ate nothing during those days, and at the end of them he was hungry" (Luke 4:1–2). Jesus was about to redeem fallen humanity through His teaching, miracles, and ultimately, His substitutionary work on the cross. It was the most important work in all of history, and it began with fasting. Recognize that Jesus conquered the greatest threat to His salvation work through fasting. Luke concludes that following the victory in the wilderness, "Jesus returned . . . in the power of the Spirit" (Luke 4:14).

Fasting to experience the Father's joy

Jesus taught His disciples to fast as a secret partnership with God their Father: "When you fast, put oil on your head and wash your face, so that it will not be obvious to men that you are fasting, but only to your Father, who is unseen; and your Father, who sees what is done in secret, will reward you" (Matt. 6:17–18). The unseen Father delights in His children who seek Him more than food. He rewards our coming to Him in our hunger and weakness, with hope in Him to sustain us. Fasting is not something we initiate and do to make God our debtor. Rather, fasting is a gift given to us for our good, that He might show His all-sufficiency to us. Fasting recognizes that food is good, but God Himself is better. Just as with hidden giving and praying (Matt. 6:3–6), God our Father is pleased to reward His children who have responded to His grace by fasting. It expresses that nothing else can satisfy our hearts but God.

Fasting to experience more of Christ

Christian fasting rests on the finished work of Christ. We do not fast for something we have not experienced but for more of the One we have experienced. This is what Paul taught the church at Philippi: "I count everything as loss because of the surpassing worth of knowing Christ Jesus my Lord. For his sake I have suffered

Christian fasting rests on the finished work of Christ.

the loss of all things and count them as rubbish, in order that I may gain Christ and be found in him, not having a righteousness of my own that comes from the law, but that which is through faith in Christ, the righteousness from God that depends on faith—that I may know him" (Phil. 3:8–10 ESV). It is not that we do not have Christ now. We do know Christ and because He is our great Joy, we long to know Him more deeply. This is how fasting helps us: it reminds us that everything else in this life, even as good as it may be, is a loss compared to knowing Christ more and more.

Fasting to grow in holiness

One of the greatest spiritual benefits of fasting is becoming more aware of our own inadequacies. Often we use food to cover our unhappiness and frustrations of life. In his book *The Celebration of Discipline,* Richard Foster[23] writes, "More than any other discipline, fasting reveals the things that control us. This is a wonderful benefit to the true disciple who longs to be transformed into the image of Jesus Christ. We cover up what is inside of us with food and other things." Fasting exposes our pain, our pride, our anger, and the ugliness of our sinful hearts. Fasting forces us to address our problems apart from the next tasty meal or relaxing beverage. Paul said, "I will not be mastered by anything" (1 Cor. 6:12). Hunger makes clear how dependent we are upon food; it is a "master" over our lives. Fasting helps rekindle a hunger for God, providing the occasion to feed upon the sweetness of Christ. Communion with Him through fasting makes it possible to find greater satisfaction in Christ than in food. Fasting is the passionate decision to resist whatever competes with your joy in Christ.

Fasting out of longing for Christ

"John's disciples came and asked him, 'How is it that we and the Pharisees fast often, but your disciples do not fast?' Jesus answered, 'How can the guests of the bridegroom mourn while he is with them? The time will come when the bridegroom will be taken from them; then they will fast'" (Matt. 9:14–15). Jesus says that fasting is like mourning, which is appropriate when someone you love is taken away. While Jesus was on earth, He was like a bridegroom at a wedding feast; all would celebrate His presence joyfully. So also, the presence of Christ on earth was too wonderful to combine with fasting. But the day would come when Jesus would ascend to heaven. At that time His people would long for His return and fast (mourn) for Him. As John Piper[24] says in *A Hunger for God,* "There is an ache inside every Christian that Jesus is not here as fully and intimately and as powerfully and as gloriously as we want him to be. We hunger for so much more. That is why we fast: because Christ has come, and will be coming again. We want to long for His return to be unhindered in our adoration and joy in His presence."

Preparing for a Fast

Clarify your purpose

Why are you fasting? Is it to deepen your love for Christ? Is it for God's guidance? For healing? For God's provision? Or for the resolution of an impossible problem? Ask the Holy Spirit to clarify His leading and purpose for your time of prayer and fasting. This will enable you to meditate on specific promises from His word and to pray more specifically.

Make a commitment

Jesus implied that all of His followers should fast (Matt. 6:16–18; 9:14–15). For Him it was a matter of when believers would fast, not if they would do it. Making a commitment before you start will keep you going when you get hungry, discouraged, or tempted to quit. Create a plan. When will you fast and for how long—one meal, one day, one week, or longer? Will you fast from all foods or restrict your diet to fruits and vegetables? Or are you fasting from other distractions to your joy in Christ, such as entertainment, media, or social networking?

Prepare your heart

Start with the assurance that God is your Father and that He loves you and is for you (Rom. 8:31–39). Confess your sin. Unconfessed sin can hinder your prayers (Ps. 66:18). Seek forgiveness from all whom you have offended, and forgive all who have hurt you (Mark 11:25; Luke 11:4; Luke 17:3–4). Ask God to fill you with His Holy Spirit (Luke 4:1–2; Eph. 5:18). Begin your time of fasting and prayer with an expectant heart (Heb. 11:6). Be prepared for spiritual opposition. Anticipate that Satan will intensify your struggle with a variety of pressures and conflicts. Also, recognize the natural battle between body and spirit (Gal. 5:16–17). You can overcome these obstacles!

Prepare yourself physically

Fasting requires reasonable precautions. Here are some common-sense tips:

- ❑ Eat smaller meals before starting a fast.
- ❑ Eat raw fruit and vegetables for two days before starting a fast.
- ❑ To avoid headaches, reduce and then eliminate caffeine prior to the fast.
- ❑ Drink plenty of water.
- ❑ Expect to get discouraged and hungry, but remember, you can overcome!

Share your experience

Connect with others who are also fasting to maintain your commitment and to find support.

Record your journey through this time of fasting and prayer by journaling your experience.

Write down the key Scriptures God is using to speak to you, the impressions you have from His Spirit, and the new steps of faith you are taking. Share with others how God is guiding and encouraging you.

Projects and Practical Applications

Commit to fasting for one day. Following the steps above, prepare to fast for a twenty-four-hour day. Begin by skipping the evening meal and continue through the following afternoon. Combine your fast with prayer and reading of God's Word. Consider giving some time in service to the poor. For the future, consider fasting on a regular basis.

Small group discussion:

1. Share with your small group about your experience in fasting. Did you fast? What was the greatest struggle? What was the greatest encouragement?

2. Share something you learned about yourself during the fast.

3. How can your group pray for you over the upcoming week?

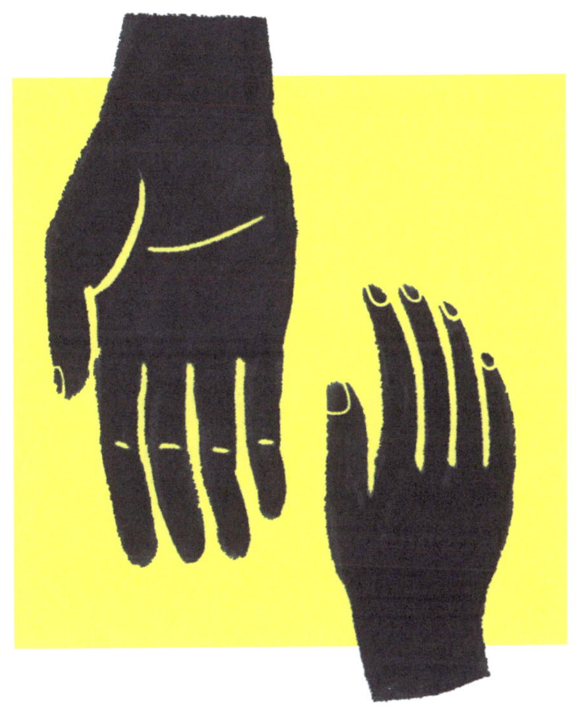

A new command I give you: Love one another. As I
have loved you, so you must love one another.
By this everyone will know that you are my disciples,
if you love one another.

John 13:34–35

7

Chapter Seven

Community

COMMUNITY

My first Christian friend was a classmate in high school named Mark. He was one year older than me, and we shared many common interests including sports, music, and girls. There was something unique about Mark; he was a Christian. He was kind to me, and he included me in his other friendships and activities. Mark also had a good relationship with his family and always encouraged me. He invited me to activities for youth with his church. One of these activities was a weekend retreat with about twelve or thirteen other teenagers and an adult youth leader. It seemed like it would be fun, so I decided to attend. The group welcomed me as if I truly belonged and made extra efforts to be kind to me. Even more impressive was the way they cared for each other. There was a feeling of love and joy among them that I had never experienced before. Throughout the weekend, we had fun laughing, playing games, and eating together. When the focus turned to worshipping God, it seemed the atmosphere became even more special. I was deeply impressed by the way they sang passionately to God, listened eagerly to Bible teaching, and discussed how this

There was a feeling of love and joy among them that I had never experienced before.

would apply to their lives. Individuals shared openly with the group about needs in their lives, and they prayed for one another with genuine sincerity and love.

During the course of the weekend retreat, the youth leader explained to me how to believe in and follow Christ. Because of the love I had experienced in this group, I had no hesitations in committing my life to Jesus Christ, and I was forever changed in a wonderful way. My first experience in biblical "community" was the setting God used to change my life. From that point forward, I have continually participated in one or more small groups of Christians who meet regularly to learn from the Bible, encourage and pray for one another, and serve together. This experience has profoundly helped me grow closer to God as well as develop the best friendships imaginable.

Vision for Biblical Community

God is in community

God the Father, God the Son, and God the Holy Spirit have forever lived in joyful unity and perfect love. In the act of creation, it was the Triune God sharing the creative work: "God said, 'Let us make . . .'" (Gen. 1:26). Before creation, God is. He eternally exists, three persons in unified Deity: "The grace of the Lord Jesus Christ, and the love of God, and the fellowship of the Holy Spirit . . ." (2 Cor. 13:14).

God the Son is also called the "Word" and enjoys close and unified fellowship with God the Father: "In the beginning was the Word, and the Word was with God, and the Word was God. He was with God in the beginning" (John 1:1–2). From eternity past, the three Persons of the Godhead have enjoyed perfect submission and eternal love for one another. God is the model of community.

God desires community with you

God loves you and desires to have a close, loving relationship with you. Moses was one who responded to God's love and experienced unusual intimacy with Him: "The Lord would speak to Moses face to face, as a man speaks to his friend" (Ex. 33:11). God longs to share close fellowship with those who respond to His grace: "If anyone loves me, he will obey my teaching. My Father will love him, and we will come to him and make our home with him" (John 14:23). God initiates an invitation for us to come and enjoy an intimate, loving friendship: "God . . . has called you into fellowship with his Son, Jesus Christ our Lord" (1 Cor. 1:9).

God created us for community with one another

God exists in community, and we are created in His image: "Let us make mankind in our image . . ." (Gen. 1:26). It is reasonable to conclude that God intends for humans to live in healthy relationships

"It is not good for man to be alone."

with one another. The first man, Adam, had unhindered access to God, perfect living conditions in the garden, and was sinless. However, God considered him lacking in relationship: "It is not good for man to be alone" (Gen. 2:18). For believers, biblical community is the supernatural quality of personal relationships made possible through the gospel and characterized by the fruit of the Holy Spirit. It is the practical application of loving one another as Christ has loved us.

The Gospel invites you into a new community

Christ entered human existence to make it possible for mankind to have a relationship with Him: "The Word became flesh and made his dwelling among us" (John 1:14). Believing in Jesus for salvation is to enter into a relationship with Him by faith. You cannot truly be a Christian apart from a personal relationship with Christ. In addition, those who experience a relationship with God through faith in Christ also enter a new depth of friendship with other Christians. The fellowship an individual experiences with Christ motivates him or her to joyfully unite with others who also know Christ (1 John 1:1–4).

The Gospel makes true community possible

God desires for His people to live in loving unity with one another. Jesus prayed the night before His crucifixion that His people would live in unity, just as He and the Father were in unity. Though sin separated us from one another, now, through the gospel, unity with others is possible: "I pray . . . that all of them may be one, Father, just as you are in me and I am in you. May they also be in us so that the world may believe that you have sent me. I have given them the glory that you gave me, that they may be one as we are one" (John 17:20–22). The forgiving grace all believers experience in Christ is the basis for their grace-filled, intimate fellowship with one another: "If we walk in the light, as he is in the light, we have fellowship with one another, and the blood of Jesus, his Son, purifies us from all sin" (1 John 1:7).

The first church was born into biblical community

God could have begun the church with one individual after another. Yet God chose to begin His church as a community of 120 believers born again simultaneously. When the Holy Spirit came at Pentecost, He created a new community where believers shared with each other what they had and experienced

God chose to begin His church as a community…

great joy in doing so (Acts 2:42–47). Their close fellowship and spiritual unity was evidence of the Spirit's leadership in their lives: "All the believers were one in heart and mind" (Acts 4:32).

Biblical community reveals Christ to the world

When Christians are united in love, support, and care for one another, it presents a powerful testimony to the world: "Let your manner of life be worthy of the gospel of Christ, so that . . . you are standing firm in one spirit, with one mind striving side by side for the faith of the gospel, and not frightened in anything by your opponents. This is a clear sign to them of their destruction, but of your salvation, and that from God" (Phil. 1:27–28 ESV).

Biblical community is the practical application of authentic faith

When we believe in Christ, the Holy Spirit produces a dramatic change in our hearts. The new love God pours into our lives has a dramatic effect on every relationship in our life. In fact, the primary environment for applying one's faith is in the family of believers (Romans 12:3–18). Genuine faith in Christ always expresses itself in loving care for one's brothers and sisters in Christ.

Characteristics of Biblical Community

Focus on Jesus Christ

Our entire existence, as well as our new birth, is entirely by the grace of the Lord Jesus Christ (Rom. 5:8; Eph. 2:8–9). Through Christ, a person is set right with God and others (Rom. 5:1; Eph. 5:1). Therefore, whenever believers come together, the central focus of their thoughts, words, and actions should be Jesus Christ (1 Cor. 2:2).

Fullness of the Holy Spirit

It is beyond human ability to produce genuine biblical community. Only when believers are yielded to the power of the Holy Spirit are we able to relate to one another as Christ intended (John 14:26; Gal. 5:22–23). The Holy Spirit produces spiritual life (John 3:3–7), leads us to unify, and to love one another (Eph. 4:4–6).

Love for one another

Because of our sinful nature, our natural disposition is selfishness. Selfishness leads to frequent conflicts and damages relationships between people. But, through the gospel, we are given freedom from selfishness and the power to love others: "Beloved, let us love one another, for love is from God, and whoever loves has been born of God and knows God. Anyone who does not love does not know

God, because God is love" (1 John 4:7–8 ESV). The quality and scope of our love for one another should reflect the sacrificial love God demonstrated for us by sending His Son to die for our sins: "By this we know love, that he laid down his life for us, and we ought to lay down our lives for the brothers. But if anyone has the world's goods and sees his brother in need, yet closes his heart against him, how does God's love abide in him? Little children, let us not love in word or talk but in deed and in truth" (1 John 3:16–18 ESV). Love should be expressed not only in attitudes and words but also in sacrificial actions and service. Love that costs nothing is not really love.

Love that costs nothing is not really love.

Christ-centered relationships

The New Testament makes clear that Christ is to be the center of all relationships between Christians. The love of Christ should saturate every relationship: "Now that you have purified yourselves by obeying the truth so that you have sincere love for your brothers, love one another deeply, from the heart" (1 Peter 1:22). Often the two-word phrase "one another" identifies a practical expression of Christ's love. Here is a list of biblical directives along with the opposite, sinful attitude or action that destroys biblical community:

Love one another . . .

- ❑ Love one another (John 13:34, 15:12) rather than hating
- ❑ Honor one another (Romans 12:10) rather than self-boasting
- ❑ Live in harmony with one another (Romans 12:16) rather than being divisive
- ❑ Agree with one another (1 Corinthians 1:10) rather than being argumentative
- ❑ Serve one another (Galatians 5:13) rather than expecting others to serve you
- ❑ Restore one another (Galatians 6:1) rather than criticizing or rejecting the one who has fallen
- ❑ Carry one another's burdens (Galatians 6:2) rather than being insensitive to others' needs
- ❑ Bear with one another (Ephesians 4:2) rather than becoming irritated or impatient
- ❑ Forgive one another (Ephesians 4:32) rather than holding grudges or becoming bitter
- ❑ Submit to one another (Ephesians 5:21) rather than defiantly reacting to leaders
- ❑ Be honest with one another (Colossians 3:9) rather than sharing superficially or dishonestly
- ❑ Warn and confront one another (Titus 3:10; Matthew 18:15) rather than avoiding conflict

- ❑ Encourage one another (Hebrews 10:25) rather than criticizing or gossiping
- ❑ Confess sins to one another (James 5:16) rather than hiding one's faults
- ❑ Pray for one another (James 5:16) rather than worrying

Shared purpose

Believers who meet together without a meaningful purpose will soon experience spiritual atrophy. Gatherings based on Christ, His active presence (by the Spirit), and His truth (Scriptures) will most likely experience genuine community (John 15:5). Biblical community requires full participation by all the believers present (1 Cor. 14:26). Participation by all is much easier when there is a clear and unifying purpose (Phil. 1:27).

Time together

Infrequent gatherings or a lack of opportunity to share vulnerably produce weak relationships. For true community to develop, believers must spend regular time together and be involved in one another's lives. We are commanded to meet together regularly for the purpose of encouraging one another toward love and good deeds (Heb. 3:13; 10:24–25). True biblical community cannot be instantly produced; it requires time to build high-quality relationships.

Threats to Biblical Community

Pride

Pride is refusal to submit to God's leadership in your life. It quenches the flow of God's Spirit and hinders our fellowship with Him (James 4:6). A proud person will demand his or her own way, live self-indulgently, and damage relationships. The acts of the flesh are listed in Galatians 5:16–21. Paul further states: "Let us not become conceited, provoking and envying each other" (Gal. 5:26).

Division

It is a contradiction of the gospel when believers are unwilling to forgive and reconcile with one another. Christians are a family of people who should be united in their love for one another: "I appeal to you, brothers, in the name of our Lord Jesus Christ, that all of you agree with one another so that there may be no divisions among you, but that you be perfectly united in mind and thought" (1 Cor. 1:10).

Self-righteousness

Because of the gospel, Christians should be the most humble and grateful people on the earth. When we wrongly believe we are superior to others, we are making ourselves equal to God as judge and denying the gospel by which we are saved. "You, therefore, have no excuse, you who pass judgment on someone else, for at whatever point you judge another, you are condemning yourself, because you who pass judgment do the same things" (Rom. 2:1). Self-righteous judging in attitudes or comments destroys true community. Jesus warned us about this in Matthew 7:1–5. (See also Gal. 2:11–16 where Paul rebukes Peter for self-righteous behavior.)

Unforgiveness

The heart of the gospel is Christ forgiving our sins through His death on the cross (1 Cor. 15:3). As God has graciously and unconditionally forgiven our sins, so we are to forgive those who have wronged or offended us: "Get rid of all bitterness, rage and anger, brawling and slander, along with every form of malice. Be kind and compassionate to one another, forgiving each other, just as in Christ God forgave you" (Eph. 4:31–32). It is especially important that brothers and sisters in Christ learn to express the gospel through the forgiveness and reconciliation they demonstrate to one another: "Bear with each other and forgive whatever grievances you may have against one another. Forgive as the Lord forgave you" (Col. 3:13).

"... forgiving each other, just as in Christ God forgave you."

Gossip

Gossip is sharing confidential information with those who are not part of the problem or part of the solution. Gossip creates further arguments: "Without wood a fire goes out; without gossip a quarrel dies down" (Prov. 26:20). Gossip damages and even "separates close friends" (Prov. 16:28). Gossip undermines trust among the community and, if left uncorrected, will permanently ruin relationships: "If you keep on biting and devouring each other, watch out or you will be destroyed by each other" (Gal. 5:15).

Superficial communication

Biblical community is about deepening relationships and focusing on meaningful personal and spiritual issues. When conversations among believers are dominated by trivial matters, it dulls one's sensitivity to the Spirit: "Do not let any unwholesome talk come out of your mouths, but only what is helpful for building others up according to their needs, that it may benefit those who listen" (Eph. 4:29). There are certain topics and issues that believers should simply avoid talking about: "Avoid irreverent babble, for it will lead people into more and more ungodliness" (2 Tim. 2:16 ESV). Arguing about theological opinions that are nonessential to salvation is a waste of time: "But avoid foolish controversies and genealogies and arguments and quarrels about the law, because these are unprofitable and useless" (Titus 3:9).

Favoritism

The gospel displays God's radical acceptance of undeserving, unworthy people. Since God through Christ accepts us, we are graciously obligated to accept others in the same way. When people feel judged or marginalized by a group of believers, it undermines the gospel we claim to believe. For instance, James provides one example that makes clear that we should not discriminate between the rich and the poor among us (James 2:1–4).

Selfishness

Christ has served us in the gospel (Mark 10:45). He has set an example that all believers should follow (John 13:15). The gospel delivers us from a self-centered life and sets us free to serve others. That is why Paul challenges believers: "Do nothing out of selfish ambition or vain conceit, but in humility consider others better than yourselves. Each of you should look not only to your own interest, but also to the interests of others" (Phil. 2:3–4). When believers lack concern for the practical and emotional needs of those in their group, it discredits the gospel (1 Cor. 11:17–22).

The gospel delivers us from a self-centered life . . .

Limited time together

"Let us not give up meeting together . . . "

Christ-centered relationships are slowly developed and must be maintained by regular involvement with one another. If people do not make the commitment to spend time together in biblical community, their spiritual lives will deteriorate: "And let us consider how we may spur one another on toward love and good deeds. Let us not give up meeting together, as some are in the habit of doing, but let us encourage one another—and all the more as you see the Day approaching" (Heb. 10:24–25).

Lack of effective church leadership

Church leaders, such as pastors and teachers, have a God-given responsibility to equip believers for unity and maturity: Christ Himself "gave the apostles, the prophets, the evangelists, the shepherds and teachers, to equip the saints for works of ministry, building up of the body of Christ, until we all attain the unity of the faith and of the knowledge of the Son of God, to mature manhood, to the measure of the stature of Christ" (Eph. 4:11–13 ESV). Like spiritual fathers, church leaders should direct the church family to respond to God's truth and serve one another as a critical aspect of spiritual development.

Unresolved conflicts

Conflicts among believers have been a reality since the beginning of the church (Acts 6:1). A shocking example from the Corinthian church was their tolerance of outrageous immorality and the deep divisions that followed: "It is actually reported that there is sexual immorality among you, and of a kind that is not tolerated even among pagans, for a man has his father's wife. And you are arrogant! Ought you not rather to mourn? Let him who has done this be removed from among you" (1 Cor. 5:1–2 ESV). When believers tolerate sin and broken relationships, it grieves the Holy Spirit and cheapens worship (Matt. 5:23–24). Unresolved conflicts are a shameful rebuke on a fellowship's spiritual immaturity: "The very fact that you have lawsuits among you means you have been completely defeated already" (1 Cor. 6:7).

Responsibilities for Biblical Community

Do your part

Every believer should take responsibility for valuing, creating, and strengthening biblical community. Where the community is suffering broken relationships, all believers should strive to restore it to health. All who believe in Christ should defend the community He died to produce.

Value biblical community

God's heart for community should inspire every member of Christ's body to be deeply committed to loving one another. Since God is love (1 John 4:7), we have our greatest intimacy with Him when we selflessly love His people. Not only do believers grow spiritually when unified with one another, but their witness to a broken and conflicted world becomes especially powerful as well: "A new command I give you: Love one another. As I have loved you, so you must love one another. By this all men will know that you are my disciples, if you love one another" (John 13:34–35). The prayer of Jesus is for complete unity among all who follow Him (John 17:21–23).

Help create biblical community

A high priority for a believer should be to continuously help form or strengthen biblical community. If biblical community does not exist, the believer should seek to create it by sharing the gospel with receptive people (Acts 16:13–15). The size of the community may be small, but Jesus promises His presence among any who gather to worship Him: "For where two or three come together in my name, there am I with them" (Matt. 18:20).

Help restore biblical community

Wherever biblical community is damaged or dysfunctional, believers should seek to bring repentance, forgiveness, healing, and restoration to all the relationships involved. The apostle Paul made this appeal to two women who were in conflict with one another: "I entreat Euodia and I entreat Syntyche to agree in the Lord. Yes, and I ask you also, true companion, help these women, who have labored side by side with me in the gospel together with Clement and the rest of my fellow workers, whose names are in the book of life" (Phil. 4:2–3 ESV). It is everyone's responsibility to restore those who have fallen out of fellowship: "Brothers and sisters, if someone is caught in a sin, you who live by the Spirit should restore that person gently" (Gal. 6:1).

. . . seek to bring repentance, forgiveness, healing, and restoration . . .

Defend biblical community

Preserving Christ-centered relationships is critically important. Therefore, it will be necessary to lovingly confront those who weaken the church or its ministry through unrepentant sin: "If your brother sins against you, go and tell him his fault, between you and him alone. If he listens to you, you have gained your brother. But if he does not listen, take one or two others along with you, that every charge may be established by the evidence of two or three witnesses. If he refuses to listen to them, tell it to the church. And if he refuses to listen even to the church, let him be to you as a Gentile and a tax collector" (Matt. 18:15–17 ESV). All Christians need to graciously protect the unity of the church by following Paul's advice to Titus: "Warn a divisive person once, and then warn them a second time. After that, have nothing to do with them" (Titus 3:10).

Biblical wisdom on friendships

Prov. 12:26 (ESV) "One who is righteous is a guide to his neighbor, but the way of the wicked leads them astray."

Prov. 17:9 (ESV) "Whoever covers an offense seeks love, but he who repeats a matter separates close friends."

Prov. 17:17 (ESV) "A friend loves at all times, and a brother is born for adversity."

Prov. 18:24 (ESV) "A man of many companions may come to ruin, but there is a friend who sticks closer than a brother."

Prov. 22:24 "Do not make friends with a hot-tempered man, do not associate with one easily angered."

Prov. 27:6 "Wounds from a friend can be trusted, but an enemy multiplies kisses."

Prov. 27:9 "Perfume and incense bring joy to the heart, and the pleasantness of one's friend springs from their earnest counsel."

Prov. 27:10 "Do not forsake your friend and the friend of your father, and do not go to your brother's house when disaster strikes you—better a neighbor nearby than a brother far away."

Prov. 27:17 "Iron sharpens iron, so one man sharpens another."

Eccl. 4:11–12 "If two lie down together, they will keep warm. But how can one keep warm alone? Though one may be overpowered, two can defend themselves. A cord of three strands is not quickly broken."

Projects and Practical Applications

1. List five specific actions you can take among your Christian friends to help strengthen biblical community.

2. Participate in a Christian small-group gathering and take note of the quality of love displayed among the relationships.

Small group discussion:

1. Describe two or three of the people God used to help bring you to faith in Christ. How did their relationship with you lead you to trust and love Jesus Christ?

2. Review the section on "Christ-centered relationships" and the accompanying list of Bible verses. Which one of the "one another" verses do you feel is most lacking in your circle of friends? Which "one another" verse do you most need from others right now?

3. Share with your group about your past week of quiet times with the Lord. Did you make time each day to meet with God in the Scriptures and in prayer? What were some of the highlights you gained from His word?

If you abide in me, and my words abide in you, ask

whatever you wish, and it will be done for you.

John 15:7 ESV

Chapter Eight

Meditation

MEDITATION

There was a particular book I had read that I found especially interesting. Therefore, when I learned that the author of the book was coming to my city for a speaking engagement, I quickly made a reservation to attend. The author's lecture was on the same themes as his book, and I was inspired by his additional insights. After the lecture, the author was available to autograph his book for the audience, and I patiently waited in the long line for this opportunity. I had many questions to ask him and envisioned a substantive conversation with this author I admired. However, when it was finally my turn to be greeted by the author, there was no opportunity to ask questions. The organizers of the event kept the line moving along, and the author quickly signed one book after another. The best one could expect was a brief, "Hello." I left the event with no meaningful connection to the author and without any of my questions answered.

Consider the contrast you can expect when approaching God and the book He wrote. Even though the Bible had many human writers, the Bible clarifies that the singular spiritual Author of the entire Scriptures is the Holy Spirit. And, if you are a believer and follower of Jesus, you have this same Author living within you. Even better, the Holy Spirit is eager to patiently teach you the meaning and applications of His truth in your personal life. This kind of interaction with the Holy Spirit is experienced through what the Bible calls "meditation."

Biblical meditation . . . leads to a deeply meaningful fellowship with the Lord.

The concept of meditation is derived from hoofed animals, like sheep and cattle. These animals have the ability to ruminate, or chew and swallow food, then later regurgitate the same food for further chewing. This process allows for more nutrition and better digestion. And, although there is a non-Christian religious exercise called "meditation" that involves clearing the mind of all thoughts and seeking to relax the body, biblical meditation fully engages the mind through intimate communion with both the written and living Word of God. Biblical meditation involves thoughtfully reflecting and prayerfully considering a portion of Scripture; it is repeatedly reviewing and continually thinking about a portion of Scripture; it is learning further insights about the truth from the Spirit, which leads to a deeply meaningful fellowship with the Lord.

Why Meditate on God's Word?

Meditation develops intimate fellowship with Him

Prayerfully reflecting upon God's Word is communicating with God in His own language. All parents know the thrill of hearing their young children speaking a word or phrase they have unmistakably learned from the parents. How much more it must bring joy to God's heart when He hears His children thoughtfully repeating His words back to Him. The life-giving nature of God's Word refreshes your heart and renews your love for Christ: "The Spirit gives life; the flesh counts for nothing. The words I have spoken to you are spirit and they are life" (John 6:63). Meditating on the words of Scripture is like welcoming God to be at home in your heart: "Whoever has my commandments and keeps them, he it is who loves me. And he who loves me will be loved by my Father, and I will love him and manifest myself to him . . . if anyone loves me, he will keep my word, and my Father will love him, and we will come to him and make our home with him" (John 14:21, 23 ESV).

Meditation prepares the way for answered prayer

Jesus promised that those who meditated upon His Word would receive answers to their prayers: "If you remain in me and my words remain in you, ask whatever you wish, and it will be given you" (John 15:7). When you delight to think deeply upon God's Word and enjoy His presence, your desires will become aligned with God's will. He is pleased to give you what you desire because it has been made consistent with His best and perfect will: "Delight yourself in the Lord and he will give you the desires of your heart" (Ps. 37:4).

Meditation brings increasing spiritual freedom

God's Word is full of life and spiritual power, so meditating upon it washes your soul and guides you to spiritual freedom: "If you hold to my teaching, you are really my disciples. Then you will know the truth, and the truth will set you free" (John 8:31–32). The more that God's Word is believed and treasured in your heart, the greater your freedom over evil: "Therefore, get rid of all moral filth and the evil that is so prevalent and humbly accept the word planted in you, which can save you" (James 1:21).

"... the truth will set you free."

Meditation renews your mind

Your mind is the focus of the sanctifying work of the Holy Spirit. He intends to transform your thinking with God's truth so that you may increasingly see life from His wise perspective: "Do not conform any longer to the pattern of this world, but be transformed by the renewing of your mind. Then you will be able to test and approve what God's will is—his good, pleasing and perfect will" (Rom. 12:2). When you choose to meditate on God's Word, you have chosen to think on what is consistent with God's truth: "Finally brothers, whatever is true, whatever is noble, whatever is right, whatever is pure, whatever is lovely, whatever is admirable—if anything is excellent or praiseworthy—think on such things" (Phil. 4:8).

Meditation equips you for spiritual battle

The mind is the spiritual battlefield for the follower of Christ. Our enemy, the Devil, seeks to fill our minds with thoughts, that, if accepted, bring spiritual defeat. We must learn to evaluate every thought, keeping what is good and rejecting whatever conflicts with God's Word: "We demolish arguments and every pretension that sets itself up against the knowledge of God, and we take captive every thought to make it obedient to Christ" (2 Cor. 10:5). God has provided our victory through the gospel, but we must learn to stand upon His victory in faith. The Word of God is the basis of our faith and our defense against the lies of the enemy: "Take . . . the sword of the Spirit, which is the word of God" (Eph. 6:17). The more we meditate on God's Word, the greater will be our spiritual victories: "I write to you, young men, because you are strong, and the word of God lives in you, and you have overcome the evil one" (1 John 2:14).

Meditation develops spiritual attentiveness

The Holy Spirit is constantly available to teach you and guide your life: "The Counselor, the Holy Spirit . . . will teach you all things and will remind you of everything I have said to you" (John 14:26). His guidance is always consistent with the Scriptures. As you meditate on God's Word, your sensitivity to God's voice increases. As someone has said, "God's voice sounds just like the Bible." His Word not only satisfies you but also creates a thirst for more: "As the deer pants for streams of water, so my soul pants for you, O God. My soul thirsts for God, for the living God. When can I go and meet with God?" (Ps. 42:1–2). Interacting with God in the Scriptures helps us increasingly understand the beautiful treasure that He is: "One thing I ask of the Lord, this is what I seek: that I may dwell in the house of the Lord all the days of my life, to gaze upon the beauty of the Lord and to seek him in his temple" (Ps. 27:4).

Meditation brings success

God promises success in everything you do if you will continually meditate on His Word: "Do not let this Book of the Law depart from your mouth; meditate on it day and night, so that you may be careful to do everything written in it. Then you will be prosperous and successful" (Josh. 1:8). True prosperity and success come from God, and He delights to give success to those who love Him wholeheartedly.

Meditation produces consuming joy

We are made to experience our greatest joy through fellowship with God. When we discover how delightful God is, we will love to meditate on His Word constantly:

"His delight is in the law of the Lord, and on his law he meditates day and night" (Ps. 1:2-3 ESV).

Meditation accelerates spiritual growth and ministry

God's Word is absolute truth: "Your word is truth" (John 17:17). The Scriptures were inspired by God and reveal who He is and how we are to respond: "All Scripture is breathed out by God and profitable for teaching, for reproof, for correcting and for training in righteousness, that the man of God may be complete, equipped for every good work" (2 Tim. 3:16–17 ESV). As you meditate on God's Word, His Spirit leads, corrects, and prepares you for greater spiritual growth. The Word of God is alive with power to transform your life: "For the Word of God is living and active. Sharper than any double-edged sword, it penetrates even to dividing soul and spirit, joints and marrow; it judges the thoughts and attitudes of the heart" (Heb. 4:12).

Meditation brings victory over temptation

When Jesus faced temptation, He responded by speaking the Scriptures, which were His meditation: "Jesus answered, 'It is written: Man does not live on bread alone, but on every word that comes from the mouth of God'" (Matt. 4:4). Meditation is "hiding" the Scriptures in your heart so that when you face temptation, you can rest in the truth as your defense: "I have hidden your word in my heart that I might not sin against you" (Ps. 119:11).

. . . you can rest in the truth as your defense.

Meditation overcomes distractions in your life

Many things, even good things, will compete for your attention. Yet nothing and no one is more deserving of your full attention than God. When you choose to focus your thoughts by meditating upon God's Word, His powerful presence will become real to you: "Be still, and know that I am God" (Ps. 46:10). This discipline is the way you direct your thoughts toward spiritual realities: "Set your minds on things above, not on earthly things" (Col. 3:2). Prayerfully reflecting upon Scripture will also enable you to mute the distractions in your life: "I have stilled and quieted my soul" (Ps. 131:2).

Meditation brings peace

When you make God's Word at home in your heart, His peace and joy will overflow from your life: "Let the peace of Christ rule in your hearts . . . Let the word of Christ dwell in you richly, teaching and admonishing one another in all wisdom, singing psalms and hymns and spiritual songs, with thankfulness in your hearts to God" (Col. 3:15–16 ESV). Guiding

"Set your minds on things above . . ."

your thoughts to align with God's Word brings lasting peace: "The mind controlled by the Spirit is life and peace" (Rom. 8:6).

Practical Steps for Meditating on God's Word

Memorize God's Word

Commit to learning the exact words of the verse and memorize it perfectly. Remember that every word of God is inspired and is profitable for your life (2 Tim. 3:16–17). The mental discipline of memorizing Scripture will be time and energy well spent.

Verbalize God's Word

"May the words of my mouth and the meditation of my heart be pleasing in your sight, O Lord, my Rock and my Redeemer" (Ps. 19:14). Believing and speaking the words of Scripture out loud is a spiritually powerful dynamic. God created the world by speaking His will (Gen. 1:3). Jesus overcame Satan's temptation by speaking forth the Scriptures (Matt. 4:1–11). God intends for you to believe and speak His Word in faith too: "Lord, open my lips, and my mouth will declare your praise" (Ps. 51:15 ESV). Salvation becomes your personal conviction when you speak your confession of faith in Christ: "For it is with your heart that you believe and are justified, and it is with your mouth that you confess and are saved" (Rom. 10:10). Believing and speaking God's Word actually strengthens your faith (Rom. 10:17). Make it your new habit to speak out loud the Scriptures you are learning.

Personalize God's Word

God's Word is a love letter to His children. Receive the words of Scripture as if God is addressing you in a personal way. He was thinking of you when He inspired the Scriptures and now wants you to recognize how His truth applies in your life. For instance, the Old Testament provides examples of how you are to properly relate to God (1 Cor. 10:1–13). Paul personalized an Old Testament law for feeding animals and applied it to his situation as one deserving financial support for his ministry (1 Cor. 9:9–11). Personalizing God's Word means quoting the verse in the first person, as if it was written just for you. For example, consider Romans 5:8: "But God demonstrates his own love for us in this: While we were still sinners, Christ died for us." To personalize it, you would say, "But God demonstrated his own love for ME, in that while I was still a sinner, Christ died for ME." Apply this same pattern to other Scriptures as appropriate, and you will gain a deeper appreciation for God's will for your life, as well as discover personal applications.

He was thinking of you when He inspired the Scriptures.

Visualize God's Word

God's Word provides many mental pictures to help you visualize the spiritual truth He wants you to understand. Jesus used vivid images in His teachings so that people could picture them in their minds (Matt. 13:3–8; 18:12–14; 19:24). Consider this striking picture of a person who meditates on God's Word: "Whose delight is in the law of the Lord, and on his law he meditates day and night. He is like a tree planted by streams of water, which yields its fruit in season and whose leaf does not wither. Whatever he does prospers" (Ps. 1:2–3). Learn to visualize yourself applying God's Word in your life; it will build your faith and determination to actually put His truth into practice.

Harmonize God's Word

Singing God's Word to Him is a special act of worship. It expresses a heart that delights in God. Even if you have no musical ability, God invites you to sing to Him. The book of Psalms is a beautiful collection of songs used by generations of worshippers. But you can use the entire Bible as your songbook to Him: "I will sing to the Lord as long as I live; I will sing praise to my God while I have being. May my meditation be pleasing to him, for I rejoice in the Lord" (Ps. 104:33–34 ESV). "Oh sing to the Lord a new song; sing to the Lord, all the earth! Sing to the Lord, bless his name; tell of his salvation from day to day.

Declare his glory among the nations, his marvelous works among all the peoples" (Ps. 96:1–3 ESV). A heart that is happy in the Lord will inevitably sing to Him: ". . . sing and make music in your heart to the Lord" (Eph. 5:19).

Projects and Practical Applications

1. As you go to sleep at night, meditate on a portion of Scripture. Focus on simply one phrase of a single verse, and think upon each word with the Lord. "On my bed I remember you; I think of you through the watches of the night" (Ps. 63:6).

2. As you have mental "free time" throughout the day, meditate on a portion of Scripture. During most days there are occasional moments of mental free time when your concentration is not needed for your task. Seize those moments as opportunities to fellowship with the Lord by meditating on Scripture.

3. Consider memorizing an entire chapter of Scripture. Memorizing a single verse is certainly helpful to your spiritual growth. However, taking larger sections or even entire chapters of Scripture brings even greater benefits because it gives you greater understanding of God's thoughts and purposes. Consider these chapters and the corresponding need each addresses:

- ❑ Psalm 23 – Comfort
- ❑ Romans 8 – Victory
- ❑ James 1 – Endurance
- ❑ Ephesians 5 – Marriage
- ❑ Psalm 139 – Security

- ❑ 1 Corinthians 13 – Love
- ❑ Philippians 4 – Joy
- ❑ Romans 12 – Relationships
- ❑ Psalm 1 – Success
- ❑ Colossians 3 – Holiness
- ❑ Psalm 91 – Protection
- ❑ John 15 – Spiritual Growth
- ❑ 1 Peter 3 – Perseverance

Small group discussion:

1. What would you consider are the three most significant distractions to your spiritual growth?

2. Describe your recent experiences with the practical steps of meditating on God's Word.

3. If you were to select a chapter to memorize or meditate on, which one would it be and why?

4. Share with the group about your past week of quiet times with the Lord. Did you make time each day to meet with God in the Scriptures and in prayer? What were some of the highlights you gained from His Word?

[He is] the Spirit of truth. The world cannot accept him, because it neither sees him nor knows him. But you know him, for he lives with you and will be in you.

John 14:17

Chapter Nine

Spirit

SPIRIT

Golf can be a frustrating game. Although I excelled at other sports as a teenager, I did not begin to play golf until my adult years. I foolishly thought I would quickly learn and master the game, but it proved me wrong. Hitting that small, white ball down the course and into the cup is enormously difficult. I purchased the best equipment, studied the instruction books, practiced tirelessly, and took lessons from professionals. Yet after a number of years of significant effort, I was only slightly better than when I began. In frustration, I finally quit altogether, recognizing that not only would I never be equal to Tiger Woods, but I had little hope of becoming even an average golfer.

. . . the expert is living within you . . .

Imagine, however, that you, an average golfer, have the finest golf professional in the world supernaturally enter your life and live within you. Because of his presence within you, your golfing abilities suddenly and dramatically improve. Now you can play golf just like the professional because the expert is living within you, providing all kinds of new wisdom for making perfect decisions. His strength and balance enable you to strike the ball with precision. Others who knew your previous golf abilities are astonished at your miraculous improvement and ask, "Why are you suddenly an expert?" "What has happened to you?" You would have to honestly answer, "It is not me; it is the expert living within me who is giving me this miraculous ability."

. . . God intends to live within you by His Holy Spirit.

This scenario is obviously a ridiculous prospect; there is no "golf professional spirit" available to help you. However, it is absolutely true that God intends to live within you by His Holy Spirit. This is why experiencing a relationship with God is unique and unlike any other relationship you have on earth. God created you, loves you, and came to save you; He also wants to live His life in you and through you by the Holy Spirit.

The Holy Spirit Introduced

He is God

The Holy Spirit is God and the third person of the Trinity (Matt. 28:19–20). There is one God in three persons: Father, Son, and Spirit, who are in continual fellowship with one another (2 Cor. 13:14). The Holy Spirit is just like Christ, but in another form: "And I will ask the Father, and he will give you another Helper, to be with you forever, the Spirit of truth . . . You know him, for he dwells with you and will be in you" (John 14:16–17 ESV).

The Holy Spirit is God's Life within each true believer, making a relationship with God possible. Jesus compared the indwelling presence of the Spirit to a river: "Whoever believes in me, as the Scripture has said, 'Out of his heart will flow rivers of living water.' Now this he said about the Spirit, whom those who believed in him were to receive . . ." (John 7:38–39 ESV).

His Attributes

As God, the Holy Spirit has all of the attributes of the Godhead. The Holy Spirit is creator (Gen. 1:2); love (Rom. 15:30); powerful (Luke 1:35); and omnipresent (Ps. 139:7–10). He guides (Luke 4:1); determines what is best for the Church (1 Cor. 12:11); and communicates with believers (Acts 8:29; 13:2).

The Holy Spirit is also a person with intellect (1 Cor. 2:10–11), emotion (Rom. 15:30, Heb. 10:29), and will (1 Cor. 12:11). He does things that a person would do, like teaching (John 14:26), speaking (Acts 13:2; Gal. 4:6), and praying (Rom. 8:26).

The Holy Spirit can be sinned against. He can be blasphemed (Matt. 12:31); resisted (Acts 7:51); insulted (Heb.10:29); lied to (Acts 5:3); grieved (Eph. 4:30); and quenched (1 Thess. 5:19).

His Names and Symbols

The Holy Spirit is called "God" (Acts 5:3–4); the "Lord" (2 Cor. 3:18); the "Spirit of God" (1 Cor. 3:16);

the "Spirit of Truth" (John 15:26; 16:13); and the "Eternal Spirit" (Heb. 9:14). He is the "Comforter" (John 14:16 ESV) and the "Helper" (John 15:26 ESV). The Holy Spirit is symbolically presented in the Bible as a dove (Matt. 3:16); wind (John 3:8; Acts 2:1–4); oil (Ex. 30:31; James 5:14); and fire (Acts 2:3).

He is the Comforter and the Helper.

The Holy Spirit in the Old Testament

Powerful and active

The Holy Spirit is present at the very beginning of creation: "Now the earth was formless and empty, darkness was over the surface of the deep, and the Spirit of God was hovering over the waters" (Gen. 1:2). God has always accomplished His purposes through His Spirit. Before the coming of Christ, He would come upon people temporarily for a specific task or initiative. For instance, the Holy Spirit is named as the one who: equipped a man with artistic abilities (Ex. 31:3–4); provided supernatural insight to prophesy (Num. 11:24–25; Num. 24:2–3; 1 Sam. 10:10); ensured military victory in battle (Judges 3:10; 6:34; 11:29; 15:14); and enabled men for governmental leadership (1 Sam. 16:13).

Though Israel tended to reject God's leadership, He sent His prophets to predict that He would one day come to live with His people in fullness, turning their hearts to Him: "I will pour out my Spirit on your offspring . . ." (Isa. 44:3). He will come to live within believers: "And I will give you a new heart, and a new spirit I will put within you. And I will remove the heart of stone from your flesh and give you a heart of flesh. And I will put my Spirit within you, and cause you to walk in my statutes and be careful to obey my rules" (Ezek. 36:26–27 ESV). The Spirit will enable supernatural experiences for whoever believes: "I will pour out my Spirit on all flesh; your sons and your daughters shall prophesy, your old men shall dream dreams, and your young men shall see visions. Even on the male and female servants in those days I will pour out my Spirit" (Joel 2:28–29 ESV). Human effort cannot save; only the Spirit of God can accomplish His salvation: "Not by might, nor by power, but by my Spirit, says the Lord of hosts" (Zech. 4:6 ESV).

The Holy Spirit in the New Testament

Christ was empowered by the Spirit

Jesus Christ came as the Incarnate God to live among men as both fully God and fully man. As God covered in flesh, Jesus humbled Himself: "Who being in very nature God, did not consider equality with God something to be grasped, but made himself nothing, taking the very nature of a servant, being made in human likeness" (Phil. 2:6–7). God the Son voluntarily "emptied" Himself and laid down His divine abilities (prerogatives) during His earthly, human life. Though He was 100 percent God while on earth and could have used His divine power at any time (Matt. 26:53), Christ chose to limit Himself by living the life of a regular man but without a sinful nature.

Jesus relied upon the Spirit and the Father for every need (John 5:19; 12:50). For instance, He needed guidance from His Father for insight when choosing His disciples (Luke 6:12). Jesus had limits to His knowledge, evidenced by the fact that He did not know when His father would establish His kingdom on earth (Mark 13:32); He could not do miracles whenever He wanted to (Matt. 13:58) because He completely submitted to His Father's will in every way, at every step (Luke 22:41–45).

Since Jesus divested Himself of His divine abilities, how did He work miracles? They were accomplished solely by the power of the Holy Spirit. At His baptism, Jesus was filled with and experienced a new empowerment by the Spirit (Luke 3:21–22), which was on full display when He was led by the Spirit to face temptation in the wilderness (Matt. 4:1). When He returned victorious from the temptations in the power of the Spirit (Luke 4:14), He preached His first public sermon in which He acknowledged that it was the Spirit who empowered Him for ministry: "The Spirit of the Lord is upon me, because he has anointed me to proclaim good news to the poor. He has sent me to proclaim liberty to the captives and recovery of sight to the blind, to set at liberty those who are oppressed, to proclaim the year of the Lord's favor" (Luke 4:18–19 ESV). From this point forward, Christ relied upon the presence and power of the Holy Spirit to do His supernatural work of ministry (Luke 5:17; Matt. 12:28).

Theologian Colin Brown[25] asserts: "The miracles of Jesus are not presented as manifestations of his personal divinity." Jesus Christ did works of supernatural power not as God, but as a man filled with the Holy Spirit. "God anointed Jesus of Nazareth with the Holy Spirit and power . . . he went around doing good and healing all who were under the power of

"God anointed Jesus of Nazareth with the Holy Spirit . . . "

the devil, because God was with him" (Acts 10:38). Therefore, the only nature Jesus used while He was on the earth was His earthly nature, not His divine nature. He was setting an example for His future believers to follow.

Christ promised the Spirit would come

"... he dwells with you and will be in you."

Jesus would only live temporarily on the earth. Yet He promised His disciples that the same Holy Spirit who was with Him would also come to them: "And I will ask the Father, and he will give you another Helper, to be with you forever, the Spirit of truth . . . You know him, for he dwells with you and will be in you" (John 14:16–17 ESV). Jesus repeatedly promised that He would send His Spirit to live within them: "When the Counselor comes, whom I will send to you from the Father, the Spirit of truth who goes out from the Father, he will testify about me" (John 15:26). The disciples must have wondered how life could possibly be better than having Jesus physically present with them day after day. Yet Jesus said it was to the disciples' advantage that He return to heaven, so that they could receive the Spirit: "It is for your good that I am going away. Unless I go away, the Counselor will not come to you; but if I go, I will send him to you" (John 16:7).

The Spirit empowered the disciples

The coming of the Spirit brought a radical transformation in the disciples' personal lives and in their purpose for living: "I am going to send you what my Father has promised; but stay in the city until you have been clothed with power from on high" (Luke 24:49). They would now be empowered to participate in His ministry to the world: "But you will receive power when the Holy Spirit comes on you; and you will be my witnesses in Jerusalem, and in all Judea and Samaria, and to the ends of the earth" (Acts 1:8).

The Holy Spirit came to the first believers approximately seven weeks after Christ was crucified and then raised from the dead. The Spirit came with great power and impact: "When the day of Pentecost came, they were all together in one place. Suddenly a sound like the blowing of a violent wind came from heaven and filled the whole house where they were sitting. They saw what seemed to be tongues of fire that separated and came to rest on each of them. All of them were filled with the Holy Spirit and began to speak in other tongues as the Spirit enabled them" (Acts 2:1–4).

The Holy Spirit's Activities

Glorifies Christ

"He will glorify me, for he will take what is mine and declare it to you" (John 16:14 ESV).

Reveals Christ

"But when the Helper comes, whom I will send to you from the Father, the Spirit of truth, who proceeds from the Father, he will bear witness about me" (John 15:26 ESV).

Convicts of sin

"He will convict the world concerning sin and righteousness and judgment" (John 16:8 ESV).

Saves

"He saved us through the washing of rebirth and renewal by the Holy Spirit, whom he poured out on us generously through Jesus Christ our Savior" (Titus 3:5–6).

Gives spiritual birth

"Flesh gives birth to flesh, but the Spirit gives birth to spirit" (John 3:6).

Unites believers to God

"He who unites himself with the Lord is one with him in spirit" (1 Cor. 6:17).

Seals

"And you also were included in Christ when you heard the message of truth, the gospel of your salvation. Having believed, you were marked in him with a seal, the promised Holy Spirit, who is a deposit guaranteeing our inheritance until the redemption of those who are God's possession—to the praise of his glory" (Eph. 1:13–14).

Justifies

"You were washed, you were sanctified, you were justified in the name of the Lord Jesus Christ and by the Spirit of our God" (1 Cor. 6:11 ESV).

Confirms adoption

"You have received the Spirit of adoption as sons, by whom we cry, 'Abba! Father!'" (Rom. 8:15 ESV).

Guarantees inheritance

"Now it is God who makes . . . you stand firm in Christ. He anointed us, set his seal of ownership on us, and put his Spirit in our hearts as a deposit, guaranteeing what is to come" (2 Cor. 1:21–22).

Baptizes into the body of Christ

"For in one Spirit we were all baptized into one body" (1 Cor. 12:13 ESV).

Provides access to God

"For through him we both have access to the Father by one Spirit" (Eph. 2:18).

Raises from the dead

"And if the Spirit of him who raised Jesus from the dead is living in you, he who raised Christ from the dead will also give life to your mortal bodies through his Spirit who lives in you" (Rom. 8:11).

Intercedes

"The Spirit himself intercedes for us . . ." (Rom. 8:26).

Inspires Scripture

"Above all, you must understand that no prophecy of Scripture came about by the prophet's own interpretation of things. For prophecy never had its origin in the human will of man, but men spoke from God as they were carried along by the Holy Spirit" (2 Peter 1:20–21).

Guides to truth

"When the Spirit of truth comes, he will guide you into all the truth, for he will not speak on his own authority, but whatever he hears he will speak, and he will declare to you the things that are to come" (John 16:13 ESV).

Empowers with gifts

"Now to each one the manifestation of the Spirit is given for the common good. To one there is given through the Spirit a message of wisdom, to another a message of knowledge by means of the same Spirit, to another faith by the same Spirit, to another gifts of healing by that one Spirit, to another miraculous powers, to another prophecy, to another distinguishing between spirits, to another speaking in different kinds of tongues, and to still another the interpretation of tongues. All these are the work of one and the same Spirit, and he gives them to each one, just as he determines" (1 Cor. 12:7–11).

Produces spiritual fruit

"The fruit of the Spirit is love, joy, peace, patience, kindness, goodness, faithfulness, gentleness and self-control" (Gal. 5:22–23).

Prepares for the return of Christ

"The Spirit and the bride says, 'Come!'" (Rev. 22:17).

Projects and Practical Applications

1. Consider how the Spirit has already been actively at work in your life. Review these Scriptures and evaluate how you have responded to the Spirit in each one:

Believing in Christ and yielding your life to Him (Titus 3:5–6)

Experiencing a close, loving relationship with God (1 Cor. 6:17; Rom. 8:15)

Allowing the Spirit to love and serve others through you (Gal. 5:22–23)

2. Reflect on how the Spirit desires to develop a relationship with you. How could you cooperate better with Him in His ministry to you?

Cooperating with the Spirit as your “Helper” (John 15:26)

Receiving the comforting counsel of the Spirit (John 14:16)

Listening for His voice to “teach you” the truth of Scripture (John 14:26)

Small group discussion:

1. Review the attributes of the Holy Spirit. Which one is most significant to you, and why?

2. Review how Christ was empowered by the Spirit. What are some of the reasons Christ chose to set aside His divine power and instead live by the power of the Spirit? What are the implications for your life?

3. Read together the Scriptures describing how the disciples were empowered by the Spirit (Luke 24:49; Acts 1:8; Acts 2:1–4). What aspects of their experiences impress and intrigue you?

4. Share with your group about this past week of quiet times with the Lord. Did you make time each day to meet with God in the Scriptures and in prayer? What were some of the highlights you gained from His Word?

But you will receive power when the Holy Spirit comes on
you; and you will be my witnesses in Jerusalem, and in all
Judea and Samaria, and to the ends of the earth.

Acts 1:8

Chapter Ten

Power

POWER

My parents were regular church attendees and insisted that all their children attend with them, as well. I went, but I did not like it; in fact, I thought it was boring and irrelevant. The music and instruments seemed outdated to me. I could not understand the pastor's sermons, so I redeemed the time by drawing pictures on scrap paper, counting tiles on the ceiling, or napping. The older I grew, the less interest I had in church. In my limited understanding, Christianity seemed to be simply a philosophy of morality, a collection of stories, and a list of rules. None of it interested me.

That was the first time I realized that God was alive . . .

My perspective changed when I heard a man speaking publicly on television about how his life had been dramatically changed by Jesus Christ. He shared how he had wasted his life in drug abuse and immorality, but that he called upon Christ to rescue him. Jesus Christ powerfully transformed his life, and this man described himself as "forgiven, free, and full of joy." That was the first time I realized that God was alive, powerful, and eager to be involved in individual lives.

Over the years, I have had much more exposure and many other experiences with God's power, which have dramatically transformed my life in so many ways. I have seen people set free from addictions, restored from deep emotional scars, and healed of physical diseases. And I have heard God speak through prophets with amazing clarity and detail about a person's secrets in order to bring powerful encouragement and hope. I have even experienced God's supernatural guidance in decision-making, in meeting financial needs, and in softening the hardest of hearts. God's goodness is incredible and His power is absolute! And I discovered that I was not alone in my experiences. In the early nineteenth century, Presbyterian minister and revivalist Charles Finney[26] had a deep experience with the Holy Spirit. He described it in this way:

> The Holy Spirit descended upon me in a manner that seemed to go through me, body and soul. I could feel the impression, like a wave of electricity, going through and through me. Indeed it seemed to come in waves and waves of liquid love for I could not express it in any other way. It seemed like the very breath of God.
>
> No words can express the wonderful love that was shed abroad in my heart. I wept aloud with joy and love; and I do not know but I should say, I literally bellowed out the

> unutterable gushings of my heart. These waves came over me, and over me, and over me, one after the other, until I recollect I cried out, "I shall die if these waves continue to pass over me." I said, "Lord, I cannot bear any more"; yet I had no fear of death.
>
> How long I continued in this state, with this baptism continuing to roll over me and go through me, I do not know. But I know it was late in the evening when a friend came into the office to see me. He found me in this state of loud weeping, and said to me, "Mr. Finney, what ails you?" I could make him no answer for some time. He then said, "Are you in pain?" I gathered myself up as best I could, and replied, "No, but so happy that I cannot live."

The Power of the Holy Spirit

The Holy Spirit intends to do two primary works of grace in your life. First, the Spirit desires to reproduce the character of Christ within you. That is, He wants you to have the same kind of motives, attitudes, thoughts, and actions that Christ would have. He comes to live within you the moment you believe and trust in Jesus Christ, and He begins this amazing transformation. From that moment forward, the Spirit continually guides you to trust and obey Him, allowing Him to fill your life with His love. Secondly, the Spirit desires to reproduce the ministry of Christ through your life. He comes upon you and empowers you for effective service. As you yield to His presence, the Spirit works powerfully through you to accomplish God's purposes. Below are further insights on these two aspects of the Spirit's work.

The Spirit Reproduces Christ's Character in You

Christ lives "within" you

> *"... your body is a temple of the Holy Spirit..."*

"I pray that out of his glorious riches he may strengthen you with power through his Spirit in your inner being, so that Christ may dwell in your hearts through faith" (Eph. 3:16–17). "Do you not know that your body is a temple of the Holy Spirit, who is in you, whom you have received from God?" (1 Cor. 6:19).

He transforms

"And we all, with unveiled face, beholding the glory of the Lord, are being transformed into the same image from one degree of glory to another. For this comes from the Lord who is the Spirit" (2 Cor. 3:18 ESV).

He creates spiritual fruit

"But the fruit of the Spirit is love, joy, peace, patience, kindness, goodness, faithfulness, gentleness and self-control" (Gal. 5:22–23).

He teaches and explains Scripture

"But the Helper, the Holy Spirit, whom the Father will send in my name, he will teach you all things and bring to your remembrance all that I have said to you" (John 14:26 ESV).

He overcomes the sinful nature

"Walk by the Spirit, and you will not gratify the desires of the flesh" (Gal. 5:16 ESV).

He liberates from sin

"For the law of the Spirit of life has set you free in Christ Jesus from the law of sin and death" (Rom. 8:2 ESV).

He motivates to godliness

"For God gave us a spirit not of fear but of power and love and self-control" (2 Tim. 1:7 ESV).

He brings peace and joy

"For the kingdom of God is . . . righteousness, peace and joy in the Holy Spirit" (Rom. 14:17).

He comforts

"... another Comforter, to be with you ..."

"And I will ask the Father, and he will give you another Comforter, to be with you forever" (John 14:16).

He leads

"Those who are led by the Spirit of God are sons of God" (Rom. 8:14).

He enables worship

"We . . . who worship . . . by the Spirit of God" (Phil. 3:3 AMP).

He reveals God's will

"We have received the Spirit who is from God, that we might understand the things freely given us by God" 1 Cor. 2:12 ESV). Paul prayed that "you may be filled with the knowledge of his will in all spiritual wisdom and understanding, so as to walk in a manner worthy of the Lord, fully pleasing to him, bearing fruit in every good work and increasing in the knowledge of God" (Col. 1:9–10 ESV).

He helps believers pray

"The Spirit helps us in our weakness. We do not know what we ought to pray for, but the Spirit himself intercedes for us with groans that words cannot express. And he who searches our hearts knows the mind of the Spirit, because the Spirit intercedes for the saints in accordance with God's will" (Rom. 8:26–27). "Pray in the Spirit on all occasions with all kinds of prayers and requests" (Eph. 6:18).

He reveals more of Christ

"I keep asking that the God of our Lord Jesus Christ, the glorious Father, may give you the Spirit of wisdom and revelation, so that you may know him better" (Eph. 1:17–19).

The Spirit Reproduces Christ's Ministry through You

Christ lives "through" you

"If the Spirit of him who raised Jesus from the dead dwells in you, he who raised Christ Jesus from the dead will also give life to your mortal bodies through his Spirit who dwells in you" (Rom. 8:11 ESV).

He expands the ministry of Jesus

"I tell you the truth, anyone who has faith in me will do what I have been doing. He will do even greater things than these, because I am going to the Father" (John 14:12).

He anoints for service

"The Spirit of the Lord is on me, because he has anointed me to preach good news to the poor . . ." (Luke 4:18).

He empowers miraculous healing

"'In the name of Jesus Christ of Nazareth, rise up and walk!' And . . . immediately his feet and ankles were made strong. And leaping up he stood and began to walk" (Acts 3:6–8 ESV).

He produces boldness

". . . they saw the boldness . . ."

"Peter [was] filled with the Holy Spirit . . . they (Sanhedrin) saw the boldness of Peter . . . they were astonished" (Acts 4:8, 13).

He communicates supernatural knowledge

"'Why is it that you (Ananias) have contrived this deed in your heart? You have not lied to men but to God.' And he fell down and died" (Acts 5:4–5 ESV).

He empowers miraculous signs and wonders

"Now many signs and wonders were regularly done among the people by the hands of the apostles . . . bringing the sick and those afflicted with unclean spirits, and they were all healed" (Acts 5:12, 16 ESV).

He brings freedom from demonic oppression

"Unclean spirits, crying out with a loud voice, came out of many who had them, and many who were paralyzed or lame were healed. So there was much joy in that city" (Acts 8:7–8 ESV).

"... there was much joy in that city."

He directs cross-cultural mission

The believers "were amazed, because the gift of the Holy Spirit was poured out even on the Gentiles. For they were . . . speaking in tongues and extolling God" (Acts 10:45-46 ESV).

He inspires prophetic messages

"Prophets came . . . and foretold by the Spirit that there would be a great famine over all the world . . . so the disciples determined . . . to send relief to the brothers living in Judea" (Acts 11:27-29 ESV).

He calls and commissions leaders

"While they were worshiping the Lord and fasting, the Holy Spirit said, 'Set apart for me Barnabas and Saul for the work to which I have called them'" (Acts 13:2).

He strategically directs mission expansion

They were "forbidden by the Holy Spirit to speak the word in Asia . . . attempted to go into Bithynia, but the Spirit of Jesus did not allow them . . . a vision [of] a man of Macedonia saying 'Come over . . . and help us' . . . we [concluded] that God had called us to preach the gospel to them" (Acts 16:6-10 ESV).

He confirms the message of the gospel

"God . . . testified to it (the gospel) by signs, wonders, and various miracles, and the gifts of the Holy Spirit distributed according to his will" (Heb. 2:4).

He gives spiritual gifts to strengthen the church

"Now to each one the manifestation of the Spirit is given for the common good . . . wisdom . . . knowledge . . . faith . . . healing . . . miraculous powers . . . prophecy . . . distinguishing between spirits . . . speaking in tongues . . . interpretation of tongues" (1 Cor. 12:7–11).

The Spirit Empowered the Early Church

In Jerusalem

God initiated a supernatural experience on the day He chose to pour out His Spirit and inaugurate the church. A gathering of Jewish believers was spontaneously filled with the Spirit and spoke in various languages and dialects they did not know. This event became the catalyst for the first massive conversion of the people who heard them, which, in turn, gave birth to the church: "All of them were filled with the Holy Spirit and began to speak in other tongues as the Spirit enabled them . . . Now there were staying in Jerusalem God-fearing Jews from every nation under heaven . . . 'we hear them declaring the wonders of God in our own tongues!'" (Acts 2:4, 5, 11).

In Samaria

Samaritans were a people of mixed Jewish heritage and idolatrous religious beliefs. Yet, the people welcomed the gospel. The new believers in Samaria lacked a complete understanding of the Spirit, so Peter and John came from Jerusalem to instruct them further. "Now when the apostles at Jerusalem heard that Samaria had received the word of God, they sent to them Peter and John, who came down and prayed for them that they might receive the Holy Spirit, for he had not yet fallen on any of them, but they had only been baptized in the name of the Lord Jesus. Then they laid their hands on them and they received the Holy Spirit" (Acts 8:14–17, ESV).

By Saul in Damascus

The glorified Christ appeared in blinding light to Saul, the chief persecutor of the church, and commanded him to end his destructive madness and believe in Him. The experience dramatically changed Saul, and it left him temporarily blind. Later his sight was restored and he received the Spirit. "Ananias went to the house and entered it. Placing his hands on Saul, he said, 'Brother Saul, the Lord—Jesus, who appeared to you on the road as you were coming here—has sent me so that you may see again and be filled with the Holy Spirit.' Immediately, something like scales fell from Saul's eyes, and he could see again. He got up and was baptized" (Acts 9:17–18). Saul immediately becomes a powerful witness (see also Acts 26:16–18).

In Judea

Cornelius was a Roman military commander of Italian descent. Although he had no Jewish background, his heart was receptive to the gospel. He and his household became the first non-Jews to spontaneously receive the Holy Spirit, evidenced by speaking in tongues and praising God: "While Peter was still speaking these words, the Holy Spirit came on all who heard the message. The circumcised believers who had come with Peter were astonished that the gift of the Holy Spirit had been poured out even on the Gentiles. For they heard them speaking in tongues and praising God" (Acts 10:44–46).

"... the Holy Spirit had been poured out even on the Gentiles."

In Ephesus

A group of twelve Gentile men in Ephesus had been exposed to some aspects of the gospel, but their understanding was deficient. When Paul instructed them more completely, they believed and were baptized in the name of Jesus. Then Paul laid his hands upon these believers and they spoke in tongues and prophesied (Acts 19:1–7).

In these five instances of receiving the Spirit, there is no discernible pattern or formula. At times there were no leaders present and the experience was spontaneous. Yet, at other times leaders were present, giving instruction, laying on hands, and offering prayers. Also, the variety of responses to the Spirit included speaking in tongues, prophesying, praising God, and even scales dropping from one's eyes. The diversity of experiences described in Acts makes clear that the Spirit comes upon people in different ways and elicits different responses. The Spirit simply came upon those who were receptive to Him.

The Spirit Empowers You for New Life

Deeper love and praise for Christ

The more you yield to the leadership of the Holy Spirit, the more your love for Christ will grow. The more you love Him, the more you want to praise Him. One of the first results of the outpouring of the Spirit at Pentecost was an overflow of praise: "We hear them declaring the wonders of God . . ." (Acts 2:11). When the Spirit fills you, He will become the center of your thoughts and the joy of your heart: "Be filled with the Spirit. Speak to one another with psalms, hymns, and spiritual songs. Sing and make music from your heart to the Lord, always giving thanks to God the Father for everything, in the name of our Lord Jesus Christ" (Eph. 5:18–20).

Boldness in evangelism

Earlier Peter was so fearful that he even denied to a slave girl that he knew Jesus (Matt. 26:69–74). Yet, once filled with the Spirit, he became astonishingly bold about Christ and began proclaiming the gospel publicly (Acts 2:14–40). This new boldness among the disciples made quite an impression upon the Jewish leaders: "They

. . . once filled with the Spirit, he became astonishingly bold about Christ . . .

saw the courage of Peter and John and realized that they were unschooled, ordinary men, they were astonished and they took note that these men had been with Jesus" (Acts 4:13). The Jerusalem church earnestly prayed for God to give them greater boldness and the results were amazing: "'Lord, consider their threats and enable your servants to speak your word with great boldness. Stretch out your hand to heal and perform signs and wonders through the name of your holy servant Jesus.' After they prayed, the place where they were meeting was shaken. And they were all filled with the Holy Spirit and spoke the word of God boldly" (Acts 4:29–31). The unmistakable result of the fullness of the Spirit is a new boldness in ministry: "Paul and Barnabas . . . [were] speaking boldly for the Lord, who confirmed the message of his grace by enabling them to perform signs and wonders" (Acts 14:3).

. . . a new boldness in ministry.

Supernatural manifestations

Signs and wonders not only characterized the ministry of Jesus, but also the ministry of the disciples (Acts 10:44–46). The amazing power of the Spirit enabled Peter to raise a woman from the dead: "Peter . . . got down on his knees and prayed. Turning toward the dead woman, he said, 'Tabitha, get up.' She opened her eyes, and seeing Peter she sat up. He took her by the hand and helped her to her feet.

Then he called for the believers and the widows and presented her to them alive. This became known all over Joppa, and many people believed in the Lord" (Acts 9:40–42).

Greater awareness of the supernatural work of God

The Holy Spirit reveals spiritual realities that are hidden from others. In Paphos, a Jewish sorcerer named Elymas opposed Paul's ministry. Paul recognized a demonic presence in the man, and he declared God's hand would blind him. The impact of this supernatural sign caused the proconsul to believe in Jesus (Acts 13:9–12).

Greater intensity of spiritual warfare

As the Holy Spirit empowers you for greater usefulness in ministry, there is a corresponding resistance from the evil one. Spirit-empowered ministry raises your level of intensity in spiritual warfare. Paul and Silas cast out a demon from a slave girl, but her spiritual freedom led to their physical suffering (Acts 16:16–24). God worked powerfully as these men overcame spiritual opposition; the result was that a strong, new church was planted in Philippi (Acts 16:25–40).

Projects and Practical Applications

The same Holy Spirit who empowered Jesus for His ministry will also empower you and all believers in the same way. How can you experience the powerful presence of the Holy Spirit in your life? Here are some helpful steps:

1. Ask the Father to give you His Holy Spirit. Jesus taught us to simply ask for the Spirit: "If you then, who are evil, know how to give good gifts to your children, how much more will the heavenly Father give the Holy Spirit to those who ask him!" (Luke 11:13 ESV). Prior to the disciples receiving the outpouring of the Spirit at Pentecost, they were seeking the Lord in prayer: The believers "joined together constantly in prayer . . . they were all filled with the Holy Spirit . . ." (Acts 1:14; 2:4).

2. Recognize there is no work you can do to cause God to give you His Spirit. Christ, with His victory on the cross, has accomplished the work God required. Now, you can simply believe God's promise and receive the fullness of His Spirit: "Did you receive the Spirit by works of the law or by hearing with faith?" (Gal. 3:2 ESV). All of the Christian life is by faith, and all you will ever receive from God will come only by faith: "For we live by faith and not by sight" (2 Cor. 5:7).

3. Ask for prayer from mature spiritual leaders. There is value in receiving grace from mature spiritual leaders: "For I long to see you, that I may impart to you some spiritual gift to strengthen you" (Rom. 1:11 ESV). God often chooses to impart His gifts to His body through Christian leaders: "Fan into flame the gift of God, which is in you through the laying on of my hands, for God gave us a spirit not of fear but of power and love and self-control" (2 Tim. 1:6–7 ESV). One of the benefits of this impartation is that it brings believers together in unity and strengthens the body of Christ: "Then they laid their hands on them and they received the Holy Spirit" (Acts 8:17 ESV). Ask a mature, Spirit-empowered leader in the church to pray for you to receive a greater impartation of God's Spirit.

Small group discussion:

1. What aspect of the Holy Spirit's work in your life are you most excited about?

2. What aspects of this study are confusing to you?

3. Ask your group to pray for you, that you can receive a greater fullness of the Holy Spirit for your life and ministry to others.

4. Share with your group about the past week of quiet times with the Lord. Did you make time each day to meet with God in the Scriptures and in prayer? What were some of the highlights you gained from His Word?

APPENDIX A

Scripture Memory

Chapter One: Grace

Ephesians 2:4–5

"But because of his great love for us, God, who is rich in mercy, made us alive with Christ even when we were dead in transgressions—it is by grace you have been saved." (NIV)

Chapter Two: Repentance

1 John 1:9

"If we confess our sins, he is faithful and just and will forgive us our sins and purify us from all unrighteousness." (NIV)

Chapter Three: Worship

Romans 12:1

"Therefore, I urge you, brothers and sisters, in view of God's mercy, to offer your bodies as a living sacrifice, holy and pleasing to God—this is your true and proper worship." (NIV)

Chapter Four: Scripture

2 Timothy 3:16–17

"All Scripture is breathed out by God and profitable for teaching, for reproof, for correction, and for training in righteousness, that the man of God may be complete, equipped for every good work." (ESV)

Chapter Five: Prayer

Philippians 4:6–7

"Do not be anxious about anything, but in every situation, by prayer and petition, with thanksgiving, present your requests to God. And the peace of God, which transcends all understanding, will guard your hearts and your minds in Christ Jesus." (NIV)

Chapter Six: Fasting

Matthew 6:16–18

"When you fast, do not look somber as the hypocrites do, for they disfigure their faces to show men they are fasting. Truly I tell you, they have received their reward in full. But when you fast, put oil on your head and wash your face, so that it will not be obvious to men that you are fasting, but only to your Father, who is unseen; and your Father, who sees what is done in secret, will reward you." (NIV)

Chapter Seven: Community

John 13:34–35

“A new command I give you: Love one another. As I have loved you, so you must love one another. By this everyone will know that you are my disciples, if you love one another.” (NIV)

Chapter Eight: Meditation

John 15:7

“If you abide in me, and my words abide in you, ask whatever you wish, and it will be done for you.” (ESV)

Chapter Nine: Spirit

John 14:17

“[He is] the Spirit of truth. The world cannot accept him, because it neither sees him nor knows him. But you know him, for he lives with you and will be in you.” (NIV)

Chapter Ten: Power

Acts 1:8

“But you will receive power when the Holy Spirit comes on you; and you will be my witnesses in Jerusalem, and in all Judea and Samaria, and to the ends of the earth. (NIV)

NOTES

A Walk with God

Author's note to the reader: Below you will find links to the pastors, theologians, and authors who have positively influenced my life and whose works I have drawn upon for this book.

1. John Piper (1946–present) Piper was the senior pastor of Bethlehem Baptist Church in Minneapolis, Minnesota, from 1980 to 2013. In 1994, the church began a ministry called "Desiring God" for the purpose of spreading "a passion for the supremacy of God in all things for the joy of all peoples through Jesus Christ." http://www.desiringgod.org/

2. Louie Giglio (1958–present) Giglio founded The Passion Movement—an outreach ministry to university students—and now serves as the pastor of Passion City Church in Atlanta, Georgia. http://www.passioncitychurch.com/2.0/#/main/latest-1/

3. D.A. Carson (1946–present) Dr. Carson is a research professor at Trinity Evangelical Divinity School. Dr. Carson also is a founding council member of The Gospel Coalition and has written or edited sixty-two books and 251 articles. http://thegospelcoalition.org/resources/name-index/d_a_carson

4. John Piper (See Note 1)

5. C. S. Lewis (1898–1963) Lewis was a novelist, poet, academic, medievalist, literary critic, essayist, lay theologian, and Christian apologist from Belfast, Ireland. He was a leading Christian thinker, often referenced by those exploring the faith. http://www.cslewis.org/resource/cslewis/

6. Jack Hayford (1934–present) Hayford was the founding pastor of The Church on the Way in Van Nuys, California, and is a prolific writer of books, hymns, and choruses. http://www.jackhayford.org/about/

7. George Mueller (1805–1898) Mueller is recognized as a man of faith and prayer who brought miraculous answers from God. http://www.prayerfoundation.org/prayer_tips_george_mueller.htm

8. Oswald Chambers (1874–1917) Chambers was a Scottish evangelist and is best known for his book, *My Utmost for His Highest.* http://utmost.org/oswald-chambers-bio/

9. Dick Eastman – Eastman is the international president of Every Home for Christ, which has given over 3.25 billion gospel messages through home-to-home distribution in 216 nations resulting in over 116 million followed-up decision cards and responses. http://www.ehc.org/about-us-dick-eastman

10. John Wesley (1703–1791) Wesley was an eighteenth-century Anglican evangelist and founder of the Wesleyan Tradition. http://wesley.nnu.edu/john-wesley/

11. Jonathan Edwards (1703–1758) Edwards was an American Puritan theologian and philosopher who led churches and ministered to American Indians. http://www.ccel.org/ccel/edwards

12. Richard Trench (1807–1886) Trench was ordained as a priest in the Church of England and published books on word studies and on prayer. http://www.christianity.com/church/church-history/timeline/1801-1900/richard-c-trench-loved-words-11630435.html

13. John Wesley (See Note 10 above)

14. George Mueller (See Note 7 above)

15. F. B. Meyer (1847–1929) Meyer, a Baptist pastor and evangelist from England, worked on both sides of the Atlantic in church ministry and inner-city missions. He authored many religious books and articles. http://www.ccel.org/ccel/meyer

16. Richard Alleine (1610–1681) Alleine was an English Puritan who became a pastor and wrote many books on prayer. http://www.puritanboard.com/f118/heaven-opened-richard-alleine-38110/

17. Guy H. King (1885–1956) King was vicar of Beckenham, London, in the Church of England and a prominent leader in the Keswick Convention, which emphasized communion with God's Spirit in prayer and world mission.

18. D. L. Moody (1837–1899) Moody was an American evangelist who founded the Moody Church and Moody Bible Institute in Chicago. He is thought by many to be the greatest evangelist of all time. http://christian-quotes.ochristian.com/D.L.-Moody-Quotes/

19. Francois Fenelon (1651–1715) Fenelon was a French Roman Catholic archbishop, theologian, and poet. http://www.ccel.org/ccel/fenelon

20. Andrew Murray (1828–1917) Murray was a noted missionary leader and author of devotional writings. http://www.ccel.org/ccel/murray

21. Dallas Willard (1935–2013) Willard, formerly a university professor, was a philosopher and award-winning author on spiritual formation. http://www.dwillard.org/biography/default.asp

22. John Piper (See Note 1)

23. Richard Foster (1942–present) Foster is a Christian theologian and author in the Quaker tradition. In 1988 Foster founded Renovaré, a Christian renewal parachurch organization.

http://www.renovare.org/files/Institute/BROCHURE12-6-12.pdf

24. John Piper (See Note 1)

25. Colin Brown (1932–present) Brown is senior professor of systematic theology at Fuller Theological Seminary, an editor, and author of many books. http://www.fuller.edu/academics/faculty/colin-brown.aspx

26. Charles Finney (1792–1875) *The Memoirs of Charles Finney,* ed. Rosell and Dupuis (Grand Rapids: Zondervan, 1989).

ABOUT THE AUTHOR

Kevin Evans is the founder of Cultivate Leadership, an organization dedicated to equipping the next generation of spiritual leaders and urban church planters, with a focus at the present time in China. He currently lives in Shanghai with his wife, Lisa, and youngest daughter, Rylie.

Kevin was previously the founding pastor of Valley Creek Church in the Dallas, Texas area where he served for eighteen years. He earned his Master of Divinity degree from Regent University and his Doctor of Ministry from Fuller Theological Seminary. Kevin and Lisa have been married since 1982 and have four children. If you would like to contact Kevin, you can reach him via the Cultivate Leadership website: https://cultivateleadership.org.

Ordering Information

Your purchase of this book will help equip future spiritual leaders in other nations. How? With each full-priced purchase, two additional copies in the indigenous language of an under-resourced nation can be published.

About Cultivate Leadership

Cultivate Leadership is a mission organization focused on growing leaders for global impact. The specific aim is to equip future leaders for urban church planting. Striving to follow the pattern of Jesus, CL creates small biblical communities focused on discipleship, which produce leaders who can reproduce others with the same character and purpose. The vision is to multiply healthy leaders and churches that positively impact nations. To order a book, or for more information about Cultivate Leadership, visit the website: https://cultivateleadership.org.